The
Food Processor
Cookbook

THE FOOD PROCESSOR COOKBOOK

MARY NORWAK

WARD LOCK LIMITED · LONDON

© Ward Lock Limited 1983

First published in Great Britain in 1983
by Ward Lock Limited, 82 Gower Street,
London WC1E 6EQ, a Pentos Company.

Text filmset in Linotron Goudy
by Tradespools Limited, Frome, Somerset

Printed and bound in Italy by Sagdos SpA

British Library Cataloguing in Publication Data

Norwak, Mary
   The food processor cookbook.
    1. Blenders (Cookery)   2. Mixers (Cookery)
    3. Food processor cookery
    I. Title
    641.5'89   TX840.B5

ISBN 0-7063-6249-7

CONTENTS

Acknowledgements
The author and publisher would like to thank Moulinex Ltd for supplying the photographs within this book.

Cover photograph by Martin Brigdale
Home Economist Jacki Baxter
Stylist Gina Carminati

Equipment for cover photograph kindly loaned by The Cocktail Shop, Elizabeth David Ltd, The John Lewis Partnership, David Mellor.

Notes
It is important to follow *either* the metric *or* the imperial measures when using the recipes in this book. Do not use a combination of measures.

All recipes serve four people, unless otherwise specified.

Choosing and Using a Food Processor

The essence of the food processor is its capacity to save time and serve as an extra pair of hands. Manual chores are over within seconds and complicated and once time-consuming recipes take on a new lease of life. Additionally, the machine is compact, having been designed to stand on a small area or work-top.

The food processor has a powerful motor base fitted with a cylindrical container and a variety of knives and shredding discs. Jobs are done according to the knife or shredder which is attached, and the motor is controlled by movement of the bowl or a button. Many food processors only have one speed, but some have two speeds controlled by the knife or attachment which is used.

Basic Technique

Follow the manufacturer's instruction book when first assembling the machine. Be sure that the bowl sits firmly on the drive shaft, and then insert the required blade or other attachment before putting food into the bowl. If a blade is used, put in the ingredients and put on the cover before activating the motor with a button or by twisting the cover (according to model). The cover cannot be removed while the machine is in operation. Be careful, however, to use the pusher when pushing ingredients through the feeder tube so that fingers, knives or spoons do not come into contact with the cutting discs. Always remove the work bowl from the motor base when taking out blades or attachments so that liquid does not spill through the centre of the bowl and accumulate round the drive shaft.

A food processor performs at its best in a series of very short operations. As it operates very quickly, care must be taken that ingredients are not over-processed. The machine must be stopped instantly when the required results are achieved. It is a good idea before starting a recipe to look carefully through the list of ingredients. Sometimes you may find that you can chop all the dry ingredients first to save washing the bowl each time. Do not overload the machine; it is best not to process more than 450g/1 lb food at a time. Be prepared to process two or three batches of ingredients, and remember to cut food to be chopped into cubes not larger than 2.5cm/1 inch. Do not chop frozen or unboned meat.

FOOD PROCESSOR ATTACHMENTS AND WHAT THEY DO

Metal Blade

All food processors are fitted with a metal blade which can be used for chopping and mixing, preparing breadcrumbs, creaming cakes and making batters and purées. It will also crush ice. The blade is strong enough to chop raw meat, vegetables, fruit, etc without the addition of liquid.

Cutting Discs

A wide range of cutting, shredding, grating and slicing attachments is available, according to model, for preparing vegetables and salads, chipping potatoes, and grating hard cheese and chocolate.

Plastic Blade

All food processors have a plastic blade which is used for making pastry and rubbed-in and one-stage creamed cakes. The blade will also smooth sauces, and prepare small quantities of bread dough. In some machines, this plastic blade selects a lower speed for these processes. The metal blade can be substituted for most recipes, according to the model chosen. If in doubt, refer to the manufacturer's instructions.

Juice Extractor

This extracts juice from oranges, lemons and grapefruit, and is useful if large quantities are to be prepared. It is available on a few models only.

Whisk Attachment

This is available on a few models for whisking egg whites and whipping cream.

Maintenance

Because it is compact, the food processor need not be tucked away in a cupboard. Keep it permanently on a work-top where it will be used many times a day for all kinds of food preparation. Keep the metal blade, cutting discs and any other attachments in a cupboard above the machine, safely out of the reach of children.

To clean, simply wipe the motor base with a damp cloth and then dry well (do not immerse in water). Wash other components in warm water and detergent, rinse and dry thoroughly.

Failures and Remedies

Pastry is 'short' and difficult to roll

This can mean that too much fat has been used, or that it has been over-mixed. A little less fat can be used than usual, and the work is done in a very short time. Rub in the fat quickly. Add the water, and only process until a ball of dough is formed, switching off immediately.

Pastry is like rubber

Water has been added too slowly and mixed in between additions. Water should be tipped into the pastry quickly and the machine switched off at once.

Cake is 'heavy'

This indicates that the flour has been mixed in too vigorously, or for too long. Process only until the flour has just been absorbed.

Food is chopped too finely

It is very easy to over-chop so that items such as nuts are ground finely instead of being chopped. Only process small quantities at a time. Work on minimum speed for a very short time.

Food sticks and is not blended

This indicates that the food processor is overloaded. Check quantities of ingredients carefully as the capacity of the machine is limited.

If the mixture sticks, stop the motor and scrape down the sides, or remove some of the ingredients and process smaller quantities. In a creamed mixture, the ingredients may be too cold.

Cream curdles

This means that cream has been over-mixed. It should be added gradually, and the machine switched off as soon as the cream has been mixed in.

Cheese packs together

Oil is pressed out from some cheeses during processing, and it is a good idea to put a little flour or bread from a recipe into the machine with the cheese during processing so that it absorbs the oil and enables the cheese to grate evenly.

Cheese sauce curdles

This will happen if the raw cheese is blended with the other raw ingredients before cooking, and it will overcook. Grate the cheese separately and add to the cooked sauce.

Icing is too soft

Ingredients in a food processor should be at room temperature; if they are too warm, processing will thin the mixture. Leave the icing to firm up before using.

QUICK TIPS

BATTER

Smooth, light, creamy batter is easily produced for pancakes, Yorkshire pudding, drop scones, etc. Fit the plastic blade and put the flour and eggs into the bowl. With the machine running, add milk slowly through the feeder tube.

BLENDING

A food processor will produce smooth soups, sauces, etc very quickly. Use the metal blade to purée vegetable soups, and the plastic blade to blend sauces. To prevent splashing when puréeing soups, strain off some of the stock before processing the vegetables, then return the stock to the purée.

BREADMAKING

A small quantity of excellent bread dough may be made in the food processor, using the plastic blade. The yeast is mixed evenly through the dough and the machine saves tiring kneading. The dough may also be returned to the machine for the knocking back stage (or second kneading) that takes place after the dough has risen the first time and before it is proved (or left to rise a second time).

CAKES

Cake mixtures are light and fluffy when made in a food processor, using the plastic blade. Cakes made by the 'creaming' method are best made as one-step cakes, using soft margarine and putting all the ingredients into the processor at the beginning of processing. Cakes made by the 'rubbed-in' method may be made with the processor if the dry ingredients and fat are first processed and liquids introduced through the feeder tube while the machine is running. Whisked sponges cannot be made in the processor.

CHOPPING

The metal blade can be used for chopping a wide range of ingredients, including cheese, chocolate, meat, fruit and vegetables. Ingredients should first be cut into small pieces. The machine chops coarsely, then very finely and finally processes into purée. Because the chopping process is extremely fast, it must be carefully controlled by operating the machine for only a few seconds at a time otherwise foods will be over-processed.

CHOUX PASTRY

The food processor makes superbly light choux pastry for éclairs, etc. When the basic mixture has been prepared and cooled it should be placed in the processor bowl with the plastic blade. The eggs can then be added one at a time through the feeder tube while the machine is running. Choux pastry made by this method is featherlight and crisp.

COOKED MEAT

The metal blade on the food processor will chop cooked meat coarsely or finely, or will reduce it to a purée suitable for spreading, and this makes economical use of small quantities of leftover meat. Fat, gristle and skin should be trimmed before processing, and the meat should be cut into small pieces.

CRUMBS

Bread, cakes and biscuits can be quickly turned into crumbs in the food processor with the metal blade. Cut or break bread, cake or biscuits into small pieces and control processing carefully to the exact coarseness of crumb required. Over-processing will result in a fine powder which is unsuitable for use in recipes.

HERBS

Fresh herbs such as mint or parsley may be quickly and finely chopped, using the metal blade. It is a good idea to chop a large quantity of herbs for storage in a refrigerator or freezer.

ICE

Crushed ice for drinks may be prepared in the processor, using the metal blade.

LEFTOVERS

There is no need to waste leftovers when a food processor is available. Cooked meat can be turned into second-day dishes or spreads; cooked vegetables with stock or gravy can be made the basis of soup as can vegetable oddments from the storage bin. Cooked fruit may be made into a purée or fool, perhaps with leftover custard or cream. Hard ends of cheese may be chopped or grated for recipes or for storage in a freezer; bread, cake and biscuits become useful crumbs for immediate use or for freezer storage.

PASTRY

Dough made in a food processor is excellent as it receives little handling. Combine flour and fat(s) in the bowl and process with the plastic blade until the mixture is like coarse breadcrumbs. Use the metal blade if fat is particularly hard and cold. Add liquid through the feeder tube with the machine switched on until the dough forms a firm smooth ball round the blade. The fat should be cool and firm, and block margarine is excellent for the purpose. Water should be ice cold and added slowly as flours vary slightly (some absorb more liquid than others), so always keep back 1–2 × 15ml spoons/1–2 tablespoons in case the dough forms more quickly than expected. Pastry made in the processor will not be warm, so should not need chilling, but it is advisable to chill flaky pastry which is a little more difficult to handle. Hot water crust pastry can also be quickly made.

RAW MEAT

Raw meat of all kinds, including offal, can be coarsely or finely chopped with the metal blade. It takes about 15 seconds to chop 450g/1lb meat evenly and finely. This processing is ideal for making burgers or steak tartare, and is invaluable when preparing pâtés.

SALADS

A food processor is a particular advantage to those wishing to vary the type and texture of salads. Raw vegetables may be chopped with the metal blade, or grated, shredded or sliced with the various discs. Cooked vegetables may be chopped coarsely for adding to mayonnaise or salad cream. All types of salad dressings may be made in the processor.

SAUCES

In addition to salad dressings, a wide variety of sauces may be prepared in the food processor. A sauce may be made by a conventional method and then smoothed in small quantities in the processor bowl, using the plastic blade. Flour-based sauces may be mixed in the processor *before* heating which speeds up the cooking and keeps the sauce smooth. Emulsified sauces, which require the slow addition of oil or melted butter, can be safely made in the processor as the liquid can be poured very slowly through the feeder tube.

Soups and Starters

French Onion Soup

450g/1 lb onions
50g/2 oz butter
1 × 15ml spoon/1 tablespoon cooking oil
900ml/1½ pints stock
salt and pepper
a large sprig of parsley
50g/2 oz Cheddar cheese
4 thick slices French bread

Quarter the onions and slice them (slicing disc). Melt the butter and oil together in a pan and stir in the sliced onions. Cook over low heat until soft and golden but not browned. Add the stock, salt and pepper, and simmer for 20 minutes. Chop the parsley (metal blade). Grate the cheese (grating disc). Toast the bread slices on one side. Sprinkle cheese on the other side, and toast until bubbling. Pour the soup into serving bowls and float a toast slice in each.

Gazpacho

900g/2 lb ripe tomatoes
2 large Spanish onions
2 cloves garlic
4 × 15ml spoons/4 tablespoons olive oil
salt and pepper
a pinch of celery salt
150ml/¼ pint dry sherry
1 × 15ml spoon/1 tablespoon tarragon vinegar

GARNISHES
1 cucumber
450g/1 lb green, red and yellow peppers
4 large ripe tomatoes
1 small loaf white bread

Cut the tomatoes in half and put into a large pan. Slice the onions (slicing disc). Crush the garlic cloves, and add with the onions to the tomatoes. Cover with water, add the oil, salt and pepper, celery salt, sherry and vinegar and bring to the boil. Cover and simmer for 1 hour. Cool and blend in small quantities (metal blade). Put through a sieve to remove pips and skin, and pour into a serving bowl. Chill for at least 2 hours before serving.

To make the garnishes, peel the cucumber and chop coarsely (metal blade). Chop the peppers coarsely (metal blade), mixing the different colours. Skin the tomatoes and remove the pips. Chop the flesh coarsely (metal blade). Remove the crusts from the bread; cut the bread into dice and bake at 150°C/300°F/Gas 2 for 5 minutes.

Put the cucumber, peppers, tomatoes and bread into individual serving dishes. Serve the chilled soup with the side dishes for garnishing.

LENTIL SOUP WITH FRANKFURTERS

350g/12 oz lentils
6 ripe tomatoes
1 carrot
1 onion
1.8 litres/3 pints bacon stock
salt and pepper
2 frankfurter sausages

Soak the lentils for 12 hours in cold water. Skin the tomatoes and remove the pips. Chop the flesh coarsely (metal blade). Chop the carrot and onion coarsely (metal blade). Drain the lentils and put them in a saucepan. Add the tomatoes, carrot and onion. Pour in the bacon stock, and add salt and pepper if required. (If the stock is very salty, do not add extra salt.) Bring to the boil, cover and simmer for 1 hour until the lentils are soft. Cool slightly and blend in small quantities until smooth (metal blade). Slice the frankfurters thickly and add to the soup. Re-heat, and season to taste.

MINESTRONE

75g/3 oz dried haricot beans
1.8 litres/3 pints beef **or** bacon stock
100g/4 oz smoked bacon, without rinds
1 large carrot
1 onion
¼ small cabbage
225g/8 oz potatoes
1 clove garlic
225g/8 oz canned tomatoes
100g/4 oz frozen peas
a pinch of dried rosemary
salt and pepper
75g/3 oz pasta

GARNISH
3 sprigs parsley
25g/1 oz Parmesan **or** Cheddar cheese

Put the beans into a bowl, cover with cold water and leave to soak overnight. Drain the beans and put them into a pan with the stock. Bring to the boil, cover and simmer for 1 hour. Chop the bacon (metal blade) and heat the pieces in a small pan until the fat runs and the bacon is golden-brown. Drain off the excess fat, and put the bacon into the stock. Slice the carrot, onion and cabbage (slicing disc). Chop the potatoes coarsely (metal blade). Crush the garlic clove and add with the vegetables to the stock. Add the tomatoes and their juice. Cover and simmer for 35 minutes, then stir in the peas, rosemary, salt and pepper; simmer for 5 minutes. Add pasta shapes or small pieces of macaroni, spaghetti or vermicelli, and cook for 10–12 minutes until the pasta is tender. Chop the parsley (metal blade) and grate the cheese (grating disc). Serve the soup in a tureen or individual bowls and sprinkle with the parsley and cheese.

Minestrone

COD CHOWDER

675g/1½ lb cod **or** haddock
600ml/1 pint water
1 large onion
50g/2 oz butter
2 large potatoes
3 celery sticks
25g/1 oz plain flour
1.5 litres/2½ pints milk
1 × 15ml spoon/1 tablespoon Worcestershire sauce
salt and pepper

GARNISH
a sprig of parsley

Cover the fish with the water and simmer for 20 minutes. Drain, retaining the cooking liquid. Remove the skin and bones, and flake the fish. Chop the onion finely (metal blade). Melt the butter in a pan and cook the onion over low heat for 5 minutes until soft and golden. Chop the potatoes and celery coarsely (metal blade). Add to the onions and stir over low heat for 5 minutes. Stir in the flour and cook for 1 minute. Gradually work in the milk and then add the flaked fish and half the reserved cooking liquid. Bring to the boil, then simmer for 15 minutes. Season with Worcestershire sauce, salt and pepper, and simmer for 5 minutes. Chop the parsley (metal blade) and sprinkle over the chowder before serving.

INDIVIDUAL CHEESE SOUFFLÉS

100g/4 oz Cheddar cheese
50g/2 oz shelled prawns
25g/1 oz Parmesan cheese
150ml/¼ pint milk
25g/1 oz plain flour
25g/1 oz butter
salt and pepper
4 eggs, separated
a pinch of paprika

Grate the Cheddar cheese (grating disc). Chop the prawns finely (metal blade). Grate the Parmesan cheese (grating disc). Put the milk and flour into the processor bowl and mix well (plastic blade). Melt the butter in a saucepan and stir in the milk mixture. Season well and stir until the mixture comes to the boil, then cook for 2 minutes. Cool slightly and return to the bowl with the egg yolks and grated Cheddar cheese. Mix until smooth, turn into another bowl and stir in the chopped prawns. Whisk the egg whites to stiff peaks and fold into the mixture. Divide between 4–6 greased individual soufflé dishes, and sprinkle with the Parmesan cheese. Put on a baking sheet and bake at 190°C/375°F/Gas 5 for 25 minutes. Sprinkle with paprika and serve at once.

BACON AND HERB PUFFS

50g/2 oz Cheddar cheese
50g/2 oz butter
150ml/¼ pint water
65g/2½ oz plain flour
2 eggs

FILLING
1 small onion
100g/4 oz bacon, without rinds
50g/2 oz mushrooms
50g/2 oz butter
40g/1½ oz plain flour
300ml/½ pint milk
1 × 15ml spoon/1 tablespoon chopped fresh herbs
salt and pepper

Grate the cheese (grating disc). Put the butter and water into a pan and bring to the boil. Tip in the flour and cook gently, stirring well, for 2 minutes. Cool for 10 minutes, then put into the bowl (plastic blade). With the machine running, add the eggs, one at a time, through the feeder tube, mixing until completely incorporated. Put the mixture into a piping bag fitted with a large plain nozzle and pipe round the inside of 4–6 greased individual soufflé dishes. Put on a baking sheet and bake at 220°C/425°F/Gas 7 for 20 minutes.

Meanwhile, prepare the filling. Chop the onion roughly together with the bacon (metal blade). Chop the mushroom (metal blade). Melt the butter in a pan and cook the onion, bacon and mushroom over low heat, stirring well, for 5 minutes. Stir in the flour and cook for 1 minute, then add the milk and continue stirring over low heat for 5 minutes. Stir in the herbs, and season to taste.

Take the soufflé dishes from the oven and spoon the bacon mixture into the centre of each puff. Sprinkle with the reserved grated cheese and return to the oven for 7 minutes. Serve very hot.

POTTED BEEF

1 small onion
450g/1 lb chuck steak
a pinch of ground mace
a pinch of ground allspice
salt and pepper
a sprig of parsley
a sprig of thyme
1 bay leaf
150ml/¼ pint beef stock
50g/2 oz butter
1 × 15ml spoon/1 tablespoon port **or** sherry
½ × 2.5ml spoon/¼ teaspoon anchovy essence

Cut the onion into eighths. Chop finely (metal blade) and put into a casserole. Cut the steak into cubes and add to the casserole with the mace, allspice, salt, pepper, parsley, thyme, bay leaf and stock. Cover and cook at 150°C/300°F/Gas 2 for 2½ hours. Leave the meat to cool in the stock, then drain, reserving the stock. Discard the herbs. Put the meat into the processor bowl with 2 × 15ml spoons/2 tablespoons stock, the butter, port or sherry and the anchovy essence. Mix until completely smooth (metal blade). Spoon into a serving dish and chill for 1 hour before serving with toast, or as a sandwich filling.

CRAB MOUSSE

300ml/½ pint aspic
25g/1 oz Parmesan cheese
225g/8 oz fresh **or** frozen crabmeat
2 eggs, separated
1 × 15ml spoon/1 tablespoon dry sherry
grated rind and juice of 1 lemon
1 × 5ml spoon/1 teaspoon tomato ketchup
4 drops Tabasco sauce

GARNISH
2 hard-boiled eggs
a sprig of parsley

Make up the aspic from pack crystals and leave until cool and just setting. Grate the cheese (grating disc). Chop the crabmeat finely (metal blade). Add the aspic jelly, egg yolks, sherry, lemon rind and juice, cheese, ketchup and Tabasco sauce. Continue processing until smooth and creamy. Tip into a bowl and leave until just beginning to set. Whisk the egg whites until very stiff and fold into the mixture. Put into a serving dish and chill for 2 hours.

Cut the hard-boiled eggs into pieces and chop finely with the parsley (metal blade). Just before serving, sprinkle the egg mixture on the surface of the mousse.

Serve with thin brown bread and butter.

PORK AND SPINACH PÂTÉ

1 bay leaf
225g/8 oz streaky bacon rashers, without rinds
225g/8 oz belly of pork
100g/4 oz back bacon
1 small onion
½ clove garlic
a sprig of parsley
1 × 2.5ml spoon/½ teaspoon fresh rosemary
1 size 6 egg
225g/8 oz spinach
pepper

Put the bay leaf in a 450g/1 lb greased loaf tin or terrine. Stretch the bacon rashers with a palette knife. Use two-thirds to line the terrine. Cut the pork and back bacon into small pieces and chop finely (metal blade). Cut the onion and garlic into pieces and add them to the meat. Process until finely chopped. Take out half the mixture and put to one side. Add the parsley, rosemary and egg, and process until the mixture is creamy. Put to one side. Put the spinach into a saucepan, cover and cook over high heat (do not add any water) for 4–5 minutes until just tender. Drain off any surplus liquid. Put into the processor bowl and chop finely (metal blade) but do not mix to a purée.

Mix the spinach with the two meat mixtures and season well with pepper. Put into the lined dish, cover with the remaining bacon rashers, then cover with a piece of foil, and a lid. Put the dish in a roasting tin containing 2.5cm/1 inch of hot water, and cook at 160°C/325°F/Gas 3 for 1½ hours. Remove from the roasting tin. Cool and weight the pork. Leave for 24 hours before turning out of the dish. Serve in thick slices with salad.

Pork and Spinach Pâté

GAME TERRINE

675g/1½ lb mixed uncooked game, skinned
100g/4 oz fat bacon, without rind
3 × 15ml spoons/3 tablespoons brandy
350g/12 oz lean pork
salt and pepper
a pinch of ground nutmeg
a pinch of dried mixed herbs
1 egg

Cut the game flesh in small pieces. Cut the bacon into pieces. Chop both coarsely in the bowl (metal blade) and tip into a basin with the brandy. Leave to stand for 1 hour.

Cut the pork into small pieces and then chop very finely (metal blade). Mix with the game, bacon and brandy. Season well with salt, pepper, nutmeg and herbs and stir in the egg until well blended. Put into a 1.4kg/3 lb greased ovenproof container and cover with a lid or foil. Put into a roasting tin containing 2.5cm/1 inch of hot water and cook at 180°C/350°F/Gas 4 for 1½ hours. Remove the lid. Remove from the roasting tin. Cool and weight the pâté. Leave for 24 hours before serving in slices with salad or toast.

Note Try to have a mixture of light and dark meat, and if little light meat is available, add a chicken joint to the game. Pheasant, pigeon, hare and rabbit are all good in a mixed game pâté.

ITALIAN HOT GARLIC DIP

5 cloves garlic
8 anchovy fillets
2 red peppers
150ml/¼ pint olive oil
150g/5 oz butter
1 × 5ml spoon/1 teaspoon lemon juice
pepper

Cut the garlic into small pieces. Cut each anchovy fillet into pieces. Cut the peppers into small pieces. Put into the processor bowl with the olive oil and chop very finely (metal blade). Melt the butter in a pan and, with the machine running, pour it into the feeder tube until the mixture is creamy. Put into a pan with the lemon juice and pepper to taste. Heat very slowly until the mixture boils and then simmer for 10 minutes until creamy. Keep hot over a table heater or hot-plate.

Serve with crusty bread and a selection of raw vegetables for dipping.

Note This hot dip is particularly good with summer vegetables such as radishes, tiny tomatoes, cauliflower sprigs, spring onions, fennel and crisp lettuce hearts.

HOT CHEESE DIP

225g/8 oz Gruyère **or** Cheddar cheese
600ml/1 pint milk
50g/2 oz plain flour
1 × 2.5ml spoon/½ teaspoon curry powder
50g/2 oz butter
2 × 5ml spoons/2 teaspoons concentrated tomato purée
salt and pepper

Cut the cheese into small pieces and then chop finely (metal blade). Mix the milk, flour and curry powder in small quantities until well blended (plastic blade). Melt the butter in a saucepan, pour in the milk mixture and cook over moderate heat, stirring well until the mixture boils. Simmer for 3 minutes, then stir in the cheese over very low heat until just melted. Remove from the heat and stir in the tomato purée and salt and pepper to taste. Keep warm on a hot-plate and use for dipping crisps or bread cubes.

PRAWN DIP

225g/8 oz shelled prawns
100g/4 oz crabmeat
225g/8 oz full-fat soft cheese
150ml/¼ pint natural yoghurt
1 × 15ml spoon/1 tablespoon tomato ketchup
1 × 15ml spoon/1 tablespoon lemon juice
salt and pepper

Chop the prawns coarsely (metal blade). Put to one side. Put all the other ingredients into the processor bowl and mix thoroughly until smooth and creamy (plastic blade). Add to the prawns and stir just enough to distribute them. Chill for 1 hour before serving with small salted biscuits.

BLUE CHEESE DIP

1 small carrot
1 onion
225g/8 oz cottage cheese
100g/4 oz Danish Blue cheese
3 × 15ml spoons/3 tablespoons soured cream
3 sprigs parsley
1 clove garlic
salt and pepper
4 drops Tabasco sauce

Cut the carrot and onion into pieces, and chop finely (metal blade). Add the cottage cheese and the Danish Blue cheese broken into small pieces, and process. Add the soured cream, parsley, garlic, salt, pepper and Tabasco sauce, and continue mixing until smooth. Season to taste and put into a serving bowl. Chill for 1 hour before serving.

Main Courses, Stuffings and Sauces

Beef Croquettes

350g/12 oz cooked beef
100g/4 oz day-old white bread
25g/1 oz pickled cucumber
25g/1 oz plain flour
150ml/¼ pint milk
25g/1 oz butter
2 × 5ml spoons/2 teaspoons chopped fresh herbs
salt and pepper
50g/2 oz hard bread
1 egg
oil for deep frying

Cut the beef into pieces and chop finely (metal blade). Discard the crusts and make the bread into crumbs (metal blade). Chop the cucumber (metal blade). Blend the flour and milk together (plastic blade). Melt the butter in a pan and stir in the milk mixture. Cook over low heat, stirring well, until thick and creamy. Mix in the meat, bread, cucumber, herbs, salt and pepper. Leave until cold and then form into eight sausage shapes. Break the hard bread into pieces and make into breadcrumbs (metal blade). Beat the egg lightly with a fork and coat each croquette first with egg, then with breadcrumbs. Fry in hot oil until crisp and brown. Serve hot with vegetables or cold with salad.

Lasagne

450g/1 lb raw lean beef
1 small onion
1 × 5ml spoon/1 teaspoon dried marjoram **or** sage
1 × 15ml spoon/1 tablespoon concentrated tomato purée
300ml/½ pint beef stock
salt and pepper
275g/10 oz lasagne
75g/3 oz Cheddar cheese
25g/1 oz butter
25g/1 oz plain flour
300ml/½ pint milk
1 egg yolk
a pinch of ground nutmeg
4 × 15ml spoons/4 tablespoons single cream

Cut the meat into small pieces. Chop finely with the onion, marjoram or sage (metal blade). Put into a pan and fry gently until the fat runs. Drain off the surplus fat. Stir in the purée and stock, cover and simmer for 1 hour, stirring occasionally and seasoning to taste.

Cook the lasagne in boiling salted water for 10 minutes and drain well.

Grate the Cheddar cheese (grating disc). Mix the butter, flour and milk for 5 minutes (plastic blade). Pour into a saucepan and bring to the boil. Reduce the heat and cook for 2 minutes, stirring well. Cool for 5 minutes. Put into the processor bowl and add the egg yolk, nutmeg, cream, salt and pepper. Mix for 5 seconds. Add half the cheese and mix for 5 seconds.

Put half the meat mixture into a greased ovenproof dish. Cover with half the lasagne and then half the cheese sauce. Put in the remaining meat and lasagne. Cover with the remaining cheese sauce and sprinkle with the remaining grated cheese. Bake at 180°C/350°F/Gas 4 for 35 minutes until golden-brown. Serve hot with a side salad.

Lasagne

STUFFED BAKED MARROW

1 marrow
2 onions
50g/2 oz lard **or** dripping
350g/12 oz cooked beef
175g/6 oz day-old white bread
150ml/¼ pint gravy
a pinch of dried sage
salt and pepper

Trim the ends from the marrow. Peel it and cut through lengthways to remove the top third. Scoop out the seeds and pith. Chop the onions finely (metal blade). Fry in a little of the lard or dripping until soft and golden. Cut the cooked meat into pieces and then chop finely (metal blade). Stir in the onion, and cook for 5 minutes. Discard the crusts and make the bread into crumbs (metal blade); mix with the onions and the meat. Remove from the heat and stir in the gravy, sage, salt and pepper. Fill the marrow with the stuffing and replace the lid. Spread the remaining lard or dripping on top, and cook at 200°C/400°F/Gas 6 for 1 hour. Serve in slices with plenty of gravy.

BEEF CRUMBLE

350g/12 oz chuck steak
1 large onion
25g/1 oz dripping
75g/3 oz plain flour
1 × 15ml spoon/1 tablespoon concentrated tomato purée
300ml/½ pint beef stock
salt and pepper
2 × 5ml spoons/2 teaspoons chopped fresh herbs
50g/2 oz butter
50g/2 oz Cheddar cheese

GARNISH
a sprig of parsley

Cut the steak into pieces and chop finely (metal blade). Chop the onion finely (metal blade). Melt the dripping in a pan and cook the meat and onion over low heat until golden-brown. Add 25 g/1 oz of the flour, tomato purée, stock, salt and pepper and a pinch of the herbs. Stir well and simmer for 5 minutes, then transfer to an ovenproof dish.

To make the crumble topping, put the butter and the remaining flour into the processor bowl and mix until like fine breadcrumbs (plastic blade). Grate the cheese (grating disc) and mix with the flour and butter. Add the remaining mixed herbs. Sprinkle the crumble on top of the meat mixture and cook at 190°C/375°F/Gas 5 for 1 hour. Chop the parsley (metal blade) and sprinkle on top before serving.

PEPPERED BEEFBURGERS IN WINE SAUCE

450g/1 lb rump steak
1 onion
salt and pepper
1 × 15ml spoon/1 tablespoon black peppercorns
1 × 15ml spoon/1 tablespoon oil
25g/1 oz butter
150ml/¼ pint red wine
1 × 5ml spoon/1 teaspoon chopped fresh herbs

Cut the steak into pieces and chop finely (metal blade). Chop the onion finely (metal blade). Mix the steak and onion together and season well. Form into four balls and then flatten slightly. Grind the peppercorns in a pepper-mill and press the pepper into both sides of the meat. Heat the oil and butter together in a frying pan and fry the meat on both sides on medium heat for 10 minutes, turning once. Drain off any surplus fat. Add the wine to the pan and scrape the pan drippings with a spoon to mix with the wine. Add the herbs, and simmer for 5 minutes.

Serve with vegetables or a salad and crusty bread.

Note For the flavour of this dish, it is most important that freshly ground pepper and fresh herbs are used.

STEAK TARTARE

450g/1 lb fillet **or** rump steak
1 small onion
1 egg yolk
½ × 2.5ml spoon/¼ teaspoon Tabasco sauce
salt and pepper

GARNISH
4 egg yolks
2 large sprigs parsley
4 anchovy fillets
4 spring onions
24 capers

Trim all fat from the steak. Cut into pieces and then chop finely (metal blade). Put into a bowl. Chop the onion finely (metal blade) and add to the meat with the egg yolk, Tabasco sauce, salt and pepper. Divide the mixture into four portions and shape into round thick patties. Place one on each plate.

With a soup spoon, make a depression in the centre of each patty, and put in an egg yolk. Chop the parsley finely (metal blade) and sprinkle on the meat. Chop the anchovy fillets by hand and place a small pile next to each patty. Trim the spring onions and chop finely (metal blade); arrange next to the anchovy fillets. Chop the capers by hand and arrange next to the onions. Chill for 30 minutes before serving.

Each person mixes the egg yolk and garnishes into the raw steak with his fork before eating.

BEEF AND BACON PLATE PIE

350g/12 oz prepared shortcrust pastry (page 75)
1 onion
225g/8 oz bacon, without rinds
225g/8 oz chuck steak
15g/½ oz plain flour
150ml/¼ pint water
salt and pepper
a pinch of dried mixed herbs
beaten egg for glazing

Divide the pastry into two pieces and roll into two circles to fit a 20 cm/8 inch pie plate. Line with one piece of pastry. Chop the onion finely (metal blade) and put to one side. Cut the bacon into pieces and chop finely (metal blade). Put into a pan with the onion and cook gently until the fat runs from the bacon and the onion is soft and golden. Cut the steak into pieces and chop finely (metal blade). Add to the bacon and onion and stir over low heat for 5 minutes until brown. Stir in the flour, and cook for 1 minute. Add the water, salt, pepper and herbs; mix well and simmer for 10 minutes. Leave until cold, and then put into the pastry case. Cover with the remaining pastry and brush with beaten egg. Bake at 200°C/400°F/Gas 6 for 30 minutes. Serve hot or cold.

ROAST LAMB WITH APRICOT STUFFING

1.4kg/3 lb boned shoulder of lamb
3 sprigs rosemary

STUFFING
100g/4 oz dried apricots
225g/8 oz day-old white bread
2 celery sticks
50g/2 oz melted butter
salt and pepper

To make the stuffing, cover the apricots with water, bring to the boil and simmer for 5 minutes. Drain, reserving the liquid. Discard the crusts and break the bread into crumbs (metal blade). Cut the celery into pieces. Cool the apricots for 10 minutes and put into the processor bowl with the celery. Chop coarsely (metal blade). Mix the celery with the reserved liquid, breadcrumbs, butter and seasoning, and use to stuff the lamb.

Tie the meat carefully so that the stuffing cannot escape. Put the joint into a roasting tin and place a rosemary sprig on top. Roast at 190°C/375°F/Gas 5 for 2 hours, basting occasionally with the pan juices. Before serving, replace the rosemary with fresh sprigs.

Note As the stuffing is richly flavoured, serve with plainly boiled potatoes rather than roast potatoes.

Roast Lamb with Apricot Stuffing

SOMERSET LAMB

900g/2lb boned shoulder of lamb
25g/1oz plain flour
50g/2oz butter
2 onions
1 clove garlic
2 large sprigs parsley
150ml/¼ pint dry cider
150ml/¼ pint stock
1 × 15ml spoon/1 tablespoon Worcestershire sauce
salt and pepper

Cut the meat into pieces and chop very coarsely (metal blade). Coat with the flour and fry in the butter until well browned. Put into a casserole with the pan juices. Put the onions and garlic into the processor bowl with the parsley and chop finely (metal blade). Sprinkle over the meat. Stir together the cider, stock and Worcestershire sauce, and season well with salt and pepper. Pour over the meat, cover and cook at 160°C/325°F/Gas 3 for 1½ hours.

Serve with baked potatoes in their jackets and chosen vegetables.

KIDNEY PUDDING

3 lambs' kidneys
100g/4oz day-old white bread
a sprig of parsley
1 × 15ml spoon/1 tablespoon shredded suet
1 egg
5 × 15ml spoons/5 tablespoons milk
1 × 2.5ml spoon/½ teaspoon dried mixed herbs
salt and pepper

Skin and core the kidneys, then chop them finely (metal blade). Discard the crusts and make the bread into crumbs (metal blade) with the parsley. Mix with the kidneys, suet, egg, milk, herbs, salt and pepper. Put the kidney mixture into a greased 600ml/1 pint pudding basin, cover with greased greaseproof paper and foil and put into a pan. Pour in boiling water to come half-way up the bowl. Cover the pan and boil for 1½ hours, adding more boiling water if needed so that the pan does not boil dry. Turn out and serve with gravy.

SAMOSAS

175g/6 oz self-raising flour
75g/3 oz shredded suet
a pinch of salt
3–4 × 15ml spoons/3–4 tablespoons cold water
175g/6 oz cooked lamb
1 small onion
1 × 15ml spoon/1 tablespoon oil
1 × 5ml spoon/1 teaspoon curry powder
salt and pepper
1 × 15ml spoon/1 tablespoon sweet chutney
oil for deep frying

Mix the flour, suet, salt and water to a firm dough (plastic blade). Roll out and cut into eight 7.5cm/3 inch rounds.

Cut the lamb into pieces and chop very finely (metal blade). Chop the onion finely (metal blade). Heat the oil in a pan and cook the onion and curry powder for 5 minutes, stirring well. Add the lamb and continue cooking for 5 minutes. Remove from the heat and season with salt, pepper and chutney. Leave until cold.

Put a spoonful of the lamb mixture into the centre of each pastry round. Pinch the edges of each round together to form a pasty shape, and seal firmly. Fry in deep hot oil for 5 minutes until the pastry is golden. Serve hot with chutney.

PORK OLIVES

4 thin slices lean pork
1 large onion
4 sage leaves
25g/1 oz butter
100g/4 oz day-old white bread
1 lemon
1 egg
salt and pepper
15g/½ oz plain flour
300ml/½ pint stock

Beat the pieces of pork very flat with a rolling-pin. Chop the onion finely with the sage leaves (metal blade). Melt the butter in a pan and cook the onion and sage for 5 minutes over low heat, stirring well. Lift out of the fat and put into a mixing bowl. Discard the crusts and make the bread into crumbs (metal blade). Add the onion. Cut the lemon in half and cut one half into quarters for garnishing. Grate the rind from the other half and squeeze out the juice. Add the rind and juice to the breadcrumbs with the egg, salt and pepper. Mix well and divide the stuffing between the pieces of pork. Roll up and tie lightly with cotton. Dust the pork rolls with the flour, and brown on all sides in the fat left in the pan. Add the stock, cover and simmer for 1½ hours. Remove the cotton from the meat. Put into a serving dish, pour over the pan juices and garnish with the reserved lemon wedges.

CHESHIRE PORK PIE

350g/12 oz prepared shortcrust pastry (page 75)
900g/2 lb lean pork
4 eating apples
salt and pepper
a pinch of ground nutmeg
25g/1 oz sugar
150ml/¼ pint dry white wine **or** dry cider
75g/3 oz butter
beaten egg for glazing

Divide the pastry into two pieces and roll into two circles to fit a 25cm/10 inch pie plate. Line with one piece of pastry. Cut the meat into pieces and chop (metal blade). Peel and core the apples and slice (slicing disc). Put half the pork into the pastry case and season with salt, pepper and nutmeg. Put the apples on top and sprinkle with sugar. Top with the remaining pork and season with salt, pepper and nutmeg. Pour over the wine or cider and dot with flakes of butter. Cover with the remaining pastry and cut a slit on top. Surround with pastry leaves. Brush with beaten egg. Bake at 220°C/425°F/Gas 7 for 15 minutes, then reduce to 190°C/375°F/Gas 5 for a further 45 minutes. Serve hot.

HOME-MADE SAUSAGES

225g/8 oz lean pork
225g/8 oz fat belly of pork
1 clove garlic
4 sage leaves
a pinch of dried thyme
1 × 2.5ml spoon/½ teaspoon salt
1 × 5ml spoon/1 teaspoon pepper

Cut the lean and fat pork into pieces. Chop the garlic. Chop the pork, garlic and sage leaves, coarsely or finely according to taste (metal blade). Add the thyme, salt and pepper, and process until mixed. Form into about 16 sausage shapes or flat patties. Chill for 12 hours before using so that the flavours blend and mature.

COUNTRY PORK

1.8kg/4 lb loin of pork
a little oil

STUFFING
1 eating apple
1 onion
6 sage leaves
75g/3 oz day-old white bread
1 egg
1 × 15ml spoon/1 tablespoon lemon juice
salt and pepper

Have the joint boned, and ask the butcher to score the skin finely. Make a slit in the meat where the bone has been removed so that the stuffing can be inserted.

To make the stuffing, peel and core the apple. Mix with the onion and sage leaves and chop finely (metal blade). Discard the crusts and make the bread into crumbs (metal blade). Add to the onion mixture and add the egg, lemon juice, salt and pepper. Mix well and insert into the meat.

Tie the joint in three of four places with string. Put into a roasting tin and rub a little oil over the skin. Sprinkle with salt and rub in. Roast at 180°C/350°F/Gas 4 for 2½ hours.

Cheshire Pork Pie

28

SAVOURY STUFFED PANCAKES

300m/½ pint milk
1 egg
a pinch of salt
100g/4 oz plain flour

FILLING
175g/6 oz cooked chicken
1 small onion
100g/4 oz button mushrooms
25g/1 oz butter
450ml/¾ pint white sauce (page 39)
salt and pepper
50g/2 oz Cheddar cheese

Mix the milk, egg and salt for 5 seconds (plastic blade). Tip in the flour and mix until smooth and creamy. Grease a 17.5cm/7 in frying pan lightly and fry eight thin pancakes. Keep warm.

To make the filling, chop the chicken finely (metal blade). Put to one side. Chop the onion and mushrooms finely (metal blade), then cook in the butter until just soft and golden. Stir in the chicken, and mix well. Add 150ml/¼ pint white sauce, mix well and season to taste. Divide between the pancakes and roll up. Arrange in a flameproof dish. Chop the cheese (metal blade) and add to the remaining sauce, stirring until just melted. Spoon over the pancakes. Grill until bubbling and golden.

PINEAPPLE GLAZED CHICKEN

1.4kg/3 lb chicken

STUFFING
1 large onion
75g/3 oz butter
175g/6 oz day-old white bread
50g/2 oz walnut halves
4 canned pineapple rings
50g/2 oz seedless raisins
1 × 2.5ml spoon/½ teaspoon grated lemon rind
salt and pepper
6 × 15ml spoons/6 tablespoons pineapple syrup from can

Remove the giblets from the chicken. Keep the liver for pâté or an omelet. Cook the remaining giblets in water to make stock.

To make the stuffing, chop the onion finely (metal blade). Melt half the butter in a pan and cook the onion over low heat for 5 minutes until soft and golden. Discard the crusts and make the bread into crumbs (metal blade). Put into a bowl with the onion. Chop the walnuts finely (metal blade) and put into the bowl. Chop the pineapple coarsely (metal blade) and add to the bowl. Stir in the raisins, lemon rind, salt and pepper. Moisten with 2 × 15ml spoons/2 tablespoons pineapple syrup and use to stuff the bird.

Put the chicken in a roasting tin and spread with the remaining butter. Roast at 180°C/350°F/Gas 4 for 1 hour. Pour on the remaining syrup and continue cooking for 15 minutes. Baste with the pan juices and continue cooking for 15 minutes, then lift the chicken on to a serving dish. Add 150ml/¼ pint giblet stock to the pan juices, heat and serve separately as gravy.

COUNTRY CHICKEN BAKE

6 chicken joints
15g/½ oz plain flour
25g/1 oz dripping
150ml/¼ pint dry cider
4 rashers streaky bacon, without rinds
2 large onions
225g/8 oz day-old white bread
100g/4 oz shredded suet
a pinch of dried thyme
1 × 2.5ml spoon/½ teaspoon grated lemon rind
salt and pepper
1 egg
4 × 15ml spoons/4 tablespoons milk

Dust the chicken joints in flour and brown on all sides in the dripping. Put the chicken joints in a greased ovenproof dish and pour in the cider. Chop the bacon coarsely (metal blade). Chop the onions finely (metal blade), and mix with the bacon. Discard the crusts and make the bread into crumbs (metal blade). Add the suet, thyme, lemon rind, salt, pepper, egg and milk and mix to a soft dough (plastic blade). Add the onion and bacon and mix until just incorporated. Cover the chicken with the dough. Cover with a piece of foil and bake at 180°C/350°F/Gas 4 for 2 hours. Remove the foil and continue cooking for 15 minutes.

Serve with gravy.

SUMMER CHICKEN CURRY

350g/12 oz cooked chicken
25g/1 oz desiccated coconut
150ml/¼ pint boiling water
1 onion
50g/2 oz butter
25g/1 oz plain flour
2 × 5ml spoons/2 teaspoons curry powder
1 × 5ml spoon/1 teaspoon curry paste
600ml/1 pint chicken stock
1 eating apple
1 eating pear
1 banana
50g/2 oz dried apricots
50g/2 oz sultanas
5 × 15ml spoons/5 tablespoons double cream
2 × 15ml spoons/2 tablespoons lemon juice
a pinch of salt

Chop the chicken coarsely (metal blade). Put the coconut into a bowl, pour on the boiling water and leave to soak. Chop the onion finely (metal blade). Melt the butter in a pan and stir the onion over low heat for 5 minutes until soft and golden. Stir in the flour, curry powder and paste and cook gently for 5 minutes. Strain the liquid from the coconut and add to the mixture with the chicken stock. Stir well until creamy and then simmer for 30 minutes. Peel and core the apple and pear and chop coarsely (metal blade). Slice the banana (slicing disc). Add the apple, pear and banana to the sauce with the chicken. Chop the apricots coarsely (metal blade), mix with the sultanas, cover with hot water and leave for 5 minutes. Drain and add to the chicken mixture. Simmer for 5 minutes. Remove from the heat and stir in the cream, lemon juice and salt. Serve hot with boiled rice, popadums and chutney.

Note This curry is also delicious if chilled and served with rice salad.

CHICKEN CANNELLONI

8 pieces cannelloni

FILLING
1 onion
1 clove garlic
100g/4oz button mushrooms
2 × 15ml spoons/2 tablespoons oil
225g/8oz cooked chicken
15g/½oz day-old white bread
25g/1oz Parmesan cheese
1 × 5ml spoon/1 teaspoon chopped fresh marjoram
1 egg
salt and pepper

SAUCE
50g/2oz butter
40g/1½oz plain flour
300ml/½ pint milk
150ml/¼ pint single cream
salt and white pepper
a pinch of grated nutmeg
25g/1oz Parmesan cheese

Bring a large pan of salted water to the boil and put in the cannelloni. Stir for a minute so that it does not stick together. Cook for about 10 minutes until just tender. Drain well and leave to cool while preparing the filling.

Chop the onion and garlic finely (metal blade). Chop the mushrooms coarsely (metal blade). Heat the oil in a pan and cook the onion, garlic and mushrooms for 5 minutes over low heat, stirring well. Cut the chicken into pieces and chop very finely (metal blade). Discard the crusts, and make the bread into crumbs (metal blade). Grate the cheese (grating disc). Stir the chicken into the onion mixture with the breadcrumbs, cheese and marjoram. Remove from the heat and work in the egg, salt and pepper. Cool and then divide the filling between the pieces of pasta. Roll up lengthways. Arrange the pasta in a buttered ovenproof dish.

To make the sauce, mix 40g/1½oz butter, the flour and milk until smooth (plastic blade). Pour into a pan, bring to the boil and simmer for 3 minutes, stirring all the time. Stir in the cream and heat gently, stirring well. Season with salt, pepper and nutmeg.

Spoon the sauce over the pasta and dot with flakes of the remaining butter. Grate the cheese (grating disc) and sprinkle it over the pasta. Cook at 190°C/375°F/Gas 5 for 30 minutes.

Serve as a first course, or as a main course with green salad and crusty bread.

CHICKEN AND MUSHROOM PIE

350g/12oz cooked chicken
175g/6oz button mushrooms
25g/1oz butter
600ml/1 pint white sauce made with chicken stock
(page 39)
a sprig of parsley
a pinch of dried thyme
salt and pepper
350g/12oz prepared shortcrust pastry (page 75)
beaten egg for glazing

Chop the chicken coarsely (metal blade). Slice the mushrooms (slicing disc). Melt the butter in a pan and soften the mushrooms for 4 minutes. Stir the chicken and mushrooms into the white sauce. Chop the parsley finely (metal blade). Add the herbs and season to taste. Put into a 1.2 litre/2 pint pie dish, cover with the shortcrust pastry and decorate the edges. Brush well with beaten egg. Bake at 230°C/450°F/Gas 8 for 15 minutes, then reduce to 190°C/375°F/Gas 5 and bake for 20 minutes.

PORTUGUESE COD

4 cod steaks
100g/4 oz streaky bacon, without rinds
1 large onion
1 green pepper
1 × 15ml spoon/1 tablespoon oil
450g/1 lb canned tomatoes
1 × 15ml spoon/1 tablespoon concentrated tomato purée
1 × 2.5ml spoon/½ teaspoon dried mixed herbs
salt and pepper

GARNISH
a large sprig of parsley

Grill the cod steaks and put them in a greased ovenproof dish. Chop the bacon coarsely (metal blade). Chop the onion finely (metal blade). Chop the pepper coarsely (metal blade). Heat the oil in a pan and cook the bacon, onion and pepper for 5 minutes until soft and golden. Add the tomatoes and their juice, the tomato purée, herbs, salt and pepper. Cover and simmer for 10 minutes. Pour over the cod and cook at 160°C/325°F/Gas 3 for 20 minutes. Chop the parsley finely (metal blade) and sprinkle on top just before serving.

STUFFED PLAICE IN SHRIMP SAUCE

4 small plaice
1 small onion
50g/2 oz button mushrooms
25g/1 oz butter
75g/3 oz day-old white bread
salt and pepper

SAUCE
25g/1 oz butter
25g/1 oz plain flour
450ml/¾ pint milk
grated rind and juice of 1 lemon
salt and pepper
100g/4 oz peeled shrimps or prawns
a sprig of parsley

Make a cut down the centre of one side of each fish. Chop the onion finely (metal blade). Chop the mushrooms (metal blade). Melt the butter and cook the onion and mushrooms gently, stirring well, for 5 minutes. Discard the crusts and make the bread into fine crumbs (metal blade). Add the onion mixture to the crumbs, and season well. Insert this stuffing into the cuts in the fish, then place the fish on a greased ovenproof dish, and bake at 200°C/400°F/Gas 6 for 20 minutes.

To make the sauce, blend the butter, flour and milk. Heat and stir over low heat until the sauce is thick and creamy. Add the lemon juice, then season to taste. Chop the shrimps or prawns coarsely (metal blade). Add to the sauce and heat through. Pour over the fish and continue baking for 15 minutes. Chop the parsley finely (metal blade) and mix with the grated lemon rind. Just before serving, sprinkle the parsley and lemon over the fish.

PLAICE FLORENTINE

450g/1 lb spinach
50g/2 oz butter
4 × 15ml spoons/4 tablespoons single cream
salt and pepper
4 plaice fillets
50g/2 oz day-old white bread
25g/1 oz Cheddar cheese

Put the spinach into a pan without additional water. Cover and cook gently for 3 minutes, shaking the pan frequently. Cool slightly and put into the processor bowl. Add half the butter and the cream and process to make a purée (metal blade). Season well. Put the purée into a greased ovenproof dish, and put the plaice fillets on top. Discard the crusts and make the bread into fine crumbs (metal blade). Grate the cheese (grating disc). Mix the crumbs and cheese and season lightly. Sprinkle on top of the fish and dot with flakes of the remaining butter. Cook at 200°C/400°F/Gas 6 for 20 minutes.

STUFFED TROUT IN JACKETS

450g/1 lb prepared shortcrust pastry (page 75)
4 × 225g/8 oz trout
beaten egg for glazing

STUFFING
1 onion
25g/1 oz butter
50g/2 oz button mushrooms
1 bunch watercress
75g/3 oz day-old white bread
1 × 2.5ml spoon/½ teaspoon grated lemon rind
salt and pepper

Roll out the pastry to a large square and cut into four lengths slightly shorter than the trout.

To make the stuffing, chop the onion finely (metal blade). Melt the butter in a pan and cook the onion for 5 minutes over low heat until soft. Chop the mushrooms finely (metal blade). Add to the onions and cook for 3 minutes. Chop the watercress finely (metal blade) and stir into the onion mixture. Discard the crusts and make the bread into crumbs (metal blade). Add to the onion mixture with the lemon rind, salt and pepper.

Skin the trout, removing the backbone, but leaving the heads and tails in place. Fill with the stuffing. Put a trout on to each piece of pastry and fold over to enclose each fish, leaving head and tail showing. Seal the edges well and brush over with beaten egg. Put on to a baking sheet and bake at 200°C/400°F/Gas 6 for 30 minutes. Serve hot or cold.

PIZZA

225g/8 oz once-risen bread dough (page 60)
olive oil
350g/12 oz Mozzarella **or** Cheddar cheese
450g/1 lb tomatoes
1 × 5ml spoon/1 teaspoon chopped fresh marjoram,
thyme **or** basil
pepper
75g/3 oz anchovy fillets

GARNISH
black olives

The bread dough should have risen until double in size. Turn on to a board and flatten into a long strip. Brush with a little oil and roll up like a Swiss roll. Repeat this process three times. Divide the dough into four pieces and roll each piece to a flat circle 17.5 cm/7 inches across. Oil four flat tins (or a baking sheet), and put the dough in them. Brush the surface with olive oil. Cut the cheese in thin slices or grate (grating disc) and arrange half on the surface of the dough. Skin the tomatoes, slice them and put on top of the cheese, then cover with the remaining cheese. Sprinkle with the herbs and pepper. Drain the anchovy fillets and arrange in a lattice on each pizza. Garnish with olives and sprinkle with a little oil. Bake at 230°C/450°F/Gas 8 for 25 minutes.

Variations

Pizza San Remo
Chop 450g/1 lb onions coarsely and cook in 50g/2 oz butter for 15 minutes. Season to taste and spread on the dough. Drain a can of sardines and place the fish on top. Garnish with black olives and bake as above.

Pizza Sorrento
Prepare the pizza as above but omit the anchovy fillets and olives from the topping. Instead, arrange 100g/4 oz sliced salami and 1 chopped green pepper on top of the tomatoes and cheese. Sprinkle with a little olive oil and bake as above.

CHEESE AND VEGETABLE FLAN

225g/8 oz prepared shortcrust pastry (page 75)
100g/4 oz carrots
100g/4 oz French beans
1 small onion
1 small green pepper
100g/4 oz back bacon
100g/4 oz tomatoes
50g/2 oz butter
salt and pepper
175g/6 oz Gouda cheese

Roll out the pastry and use to line a 20 cm/8 inch flan tin. Slice the carrots and beans (slicing disc). Chop the onion, pepper and bacon finely (metal blade). Skin the tomatoes and remove the pips. Chop the flesh coarsely (metal blade). Melt the butter in a pan and cook the bacon and vegetables for 10 minutes over low heat, stirring well. Season with salt and pepper and leave until cold. Put into the pastry case and cover the vegetables with a piece of foil. Bake at 200°C/400°F/Gas 6 for 45 minutes. Grate the cheese (grating disc). Remove the foil and sprinkle the cheese all over the vegetables. Continue baking for 15 minutes until the cheese has melted. Serve at once.

APPLE AND RAISIN STUFFING

2 dessert apples
50g/2 oz seedless raisins
50g/2 oz hazelnuts
100g/4 oz fresh white bread
2 × 15ml spoons/2 tablespoons golden syrup
2 × 5ml spoons/2 teaspoons oil
1 × 5ml spoon/1 teaspoon made mustard
a squeeze of lemon juice
salt and pepper

Peel the apples and cut them into quarters. Put into the processor with the raisins and nuts and chop finely (metal blade). Put into a bowl. Discard the crusts and make the bread into crumbs (metal blade). Add to the chopped fruit and nuts. Warm together the syrup and oil and add to the dry ingredients with the mustard, lemon juice and seasoning. Mix lightly and use to stuff pork, lamb or veal.

Note This stuffing is also good with rich poultry such as goose or duck.

GOOSEBERRY SAUCE

225g/8 oz green gooseberries
2 × 15ml spoons/2 tablespoons water
25g/1 oz butter
25g/1 oz sugar
a pinch of ground allspice

Chop the gooseberries finely (metal blade). Put into a pan with the water and simmer for 5 minutes. Cool slightly. Mix with the butter, sugar and spice until smooth (plastic blade). Return to a clean pan and re-heat.
Serve with mackerel or other oily fish.

SAUSAGE STUFFING

50g/2 oz streaky bacon, without rinds
chicken liver
1 onion
25g/1 oz butter
50g/2 oz fresh white bread
1 egg
450g/1 lb pork sausage-meat
2 × 5ml spoons/2 teaspoons fresh mixed herbs
stock
salt and pepper

Chop the bacon and liver finely (metal blade). Chop the onion finely (metal blade). Melt the butter in a pan and fry the bacon and liver until soft but not coloured. Make crumbs from the bread (metal blade). Mix all the ingredients, including the pan juices, egg, and enough stock to cover, with the sausage-meat in the processor bowl. Use for chicken or turkey.

CHESTNUT STUFFING

450g/1 lb chestnuts
milk
50g/2 oz day-old bread
25g/1 oz melted butter
2 × 5ml spoons/2 teaspoons fresh mixed herbs
2 eggs
salt and pepper
a pinch of mustard powder

Split the chestnuts and boil them in water for 10 minutes. Remove and discard the skin and process the chestnuts until finely chopped (metal blade). Add just enough milk to cover, and cook until tender. Cut the bread into small pieces, add to the chestnuts with the butter, herbs, eggs and seasoning, and process until well mixed (metal blade).
Use for chicken or turkey, but double the quantity for a large turkey.

HOLLANDAISE SAUCE

3 egg yolks
1 × 15ml spoon/1 tablespoon lemon juice
1 × 15ml spoon/1 tablespoon warm water
salt and white pepper
100g/4oz unsalted butter

Mix the egg yolks, lemon juice, water, salt and pepper until just blended (plastic blade). Melt the butter without browning. With the machine running, pour the butter slowly through the feeder tube until completely mixed in and the sauce is thick.

Serve immediately with fish, asparagus, artichokes or other vegetables.

Variations

Aurora Sauce
Fold 3 × 15ml spoons/3 tablespoons mayonnaise and 150ml/¼pint whipped cream into the Hollandaise sauce. Serve with cold chicken or fish.

Maltaise Sauce
Stir in 1 × 5ml spoon/1 teaspoon grated orange rind and 1 × 15ml spoon/1 tablespoon orange juice and serve with vegetables.

Mousseline Sauce
Before preparing the Hollandaise Sauce, whip 150ml/¼pint double cream to soft peaks and put on one side. Prepare the sauce and fold in the cream. Serve with fish, vegetables or eggs.

RICH BROWN SAUCE

2 rashers streaky bacon, without rinds
1 onion
1 celery stick
1 carrot
4 large mushrooms
2 × 15ml spoons/2 tablespoons oil
25g/1oz plain flour
450ml/¾pint beef stock
2 × 15ml spoons/2 tablespoons concentrated tomato
purée
1 bay leaf
a sprig of parsley
salt and pepper

Chop the bacon finely (metal blade). Chop the onion finely (metal blade). Chop the celery, carrot and mushrooms finely (metal blade). Heat the oil in a pan and cook the bacon and vegetables over low heat until the onions are soft and golden. Add the flour and stir well for 2 minutes over low heat. Add the stock gradually and then the remaining ingredients. Bring to the boil, cover and simmer for 45 minutes. Remove the bay leaf and parsley. Blend the sauce in small quantities until smooth (plastic blade). Return to the pan and simmer for 10 minutes.

Use for meat dishes.

SPAGHETTI SAUCE

1 onion
1 clove garlic
2 × 15ml spoons/2 tablespoons oil
1 carrot
675g/1½ lb chuck steak
1 chicken liver
100g/4 oz button mushrooms
25g/1 oz plain flour
225g/8 oz canned tomatoes
300ml/½ pint beef stock
4 × 15ml spoons/4 tablespoons red wine
4 × 15ml spoons/4 tablespoons concentrated tomato
purée
1 × 2.5ml spoon/½ teaspoon dried mixed herbs
salt and pepper

Chop the onion and garlic finely (metal blade). Heat the oil in a pan and cook the onion and garlic until soft and golden. Chop the carrot finely (metal blade). Add to the onion and cook for 3 minutes. Cut the steak and liver into pieces and chop finely (metal blade). Add to the pan and continue cooking until lightly browned. Chop the mushrooms finely (metal blade). Add to the pan and cook for 2 minutes. Drain off surplus fat from the pan. Work in the flour and cook for 1 minute. Drain the tomatoes and add the juice to the pan. Remove the pips, chop the flesh finely (metal blade) and add to the pan. Stir in the remaining ingredients and bring to the boil. Cover and simmer for 1 hour.
    Serve with any pasta.

TOMATO SAUCE

1 onion
1 clove garlic
1 × 15ml spoon/1 tablespoon oil
25g/1 oz plain flour
450g/1 lb canned tomatoes
1 × 5ml spoon/1 teaspoon salt
1 × 5ml spoon/1 teaspoon sugar
1 × 15ml spoon/1 tablespoon vinegar
1 × 15ml spoon/1 tablespoon concentrated tomato purée
a pinch of dried mixed herbs
1 bay leaf
a pinch of pepper

Chop the onion and garlic finely (metal blade). Heat the oil in a pan and cook the onion and garlic until soft and golden. Work in the flour and cook for 1 minute. Put into the processor bowl. Sieve the tomatoes and their juice and add to the bowl with the salt, sugar, vinegar, tomato purée and herbs. Mix until smooth (plastic blade). Put into a pan with the bay leaf and pepper and stir over low heat for 10 minutes. Remove the bay leaf and season to taste.

WHITE SAUCE

25g/1 oz melted butter
25g/1 oz plain flour
300ml/½ pint milk
salt and white pepper

Mix the butter, flour and milk until smooth (plastic blade). Pour into a pan, bring to the boil and simmer for 3 minutes, stirring all the time. Season to taste.

Variations
Prepare the ingredients in the processor before making the sauce.
Cheese Sauce
Stir 75g/3 oz grated or chopped cheese into the sauce just before serving.
Egg Sauce
Stir 2 chopped hard-boiled eggs into the cooked sauce.
Onion Sauce
Cook 1 finely chopped medium onion in the sauce. Flavour with a pinch of ground nutmeg.
Parsley Sauce
Stir 2 large chopped sprigs of parsley into the cooked sauce.
Shrimp Sauce
Add 75g/3 oz peeled, finely chopped shrimps to the cooked sauce and season with a few drops of Tabasco sauce.

WINE AND MUSHROOM SAUCE

1 onion
15g/½ oz butter
175g/6 oz button mushrooms
300ml/½ pint stock
150ml/¼ pint red wine
1 × 15ml spoon/1 tablespoon Worcestershire sauce
15g/½ oz cornflour
1 × 15ml spoon/1 tablespoon water
salt and pepper

Chop the onion finely (metal blade). Melt the butter and cook the onion until soft and golden. Chop the mushrooms finely (metal blade). Add to the onion and stir over low heat for 2 minutes. Add the stock, wine and Worcestershire sauce, stir well and simmer for 10 minutes. Cool slightly and return to the processor bowl. Mix the cornflour with the water and add to the bowl. Add salt and pepper, and mix until smooth (plastic blade). Return to the pan and simmer for 5 minutes.

Serve with steak or roast beef.

Vegetables, Salads and Dressings

Glazed Carrots

450g/1 lb carrots
300ml/½ pint chicken stock
25g/1 oz butter
2 × 5ml spoons/2 teaspoons sugar
a pinch of salt

GARNISH
a sprig of parsley

Slice the carrots (slicing disc). Put into a pan with the other ingredients except the parsley. Bring to the boil, cover and cook for 5 minutes. Remove the lid and simmer until tender and the stock is absorbed. Chop the parsley (metal blade) and sprinkle over the carrots.

Lentil Purée

450g/1 lb lentils
1 potato
1 onion
1 carrot
600ml/1 pint bacon stock
1 bay leaf
a sprig of thyme **or** marjoram
50g/2 oz butter
6 × 15ml spoons/6 tablespoons single cream
pepper

Soak the lentils for 12 hours in cold water. Drain, and put into the processor bowl. Chop finely (metal blade). Put into a saucepan. Chop the potato, onion and carrot coarsely (metal blade). Add to the pan with the bacon stock, bay leaf, thyme or marjoram. Bring to the boil, then cover and simmer for 1 hour when the liquid should be almost absorbed. Drain well and remove the herbs. Cool slightly and blend in small quantities until smooth (plastic blade). Add the butter and cream and blend again until completely mixed. Return to a clean saucepan and heat through. Season to taste with pepper.

Note By processing the lentils and vegetables first, the cooking time is shortened considerably. The potato will remove excess saltiness from the bacon stock.

SWISS POTATO CAKE

900g/2 lb potatoes
1 onion
75g/3 oz butter
50g/2 oz Gruyère cheese
salt and pepper

Parboil the potatoes in their skins for 10 minutes. Cool, then peel. Cut into large pieces and grate (grating disc). Chop the onion finely (metal blade). Melt half the butter in a pan and cook the onion for 5 minutes until soft. Add the remaining butter and then the potatoes. Grate the cheese (grating disc) and add to the mixture. Season and stir well. Press the mixture down firmly with a palette knife and cook for about 10 minutes until golden-brown underneath. Turn the potato cake over carefully with a fish slice and continue cooking for 10 minutes. Serve cut into wedges.

GREEK MUSHROOMS

450g/1 lb button mushrooms
100g/4 oz onions
4 × 15ml spoons/4 tablespoons olive oil
150ml/¼ pint white wine
juice of 1 lemon
a sprig of parsley
a sprig of thyme
1 bay leaf
a pinch of salt
a few grains coriander
4 white peppercorns

Slice the mushrooms (slicing disc). Chop the onions finely (metal blade). Heat the oil and cook the onions over low heat for 5 minutes, stirring well. Add the mushrooms and the wine. Add the lemon juice to the pan, then add the herbs, salt, coriander and peppercorns, and bring to the boil. Cover and simmer for 6 minutes. Remove the lid and continue simmering for 4 minutes. Remove the herbs and peppercorns. Transfer to a serving dish and chill for 2 hours. Serve with crusty bread.

RATATOUILLE

4 large tomatoes
2 aubergines
1 large green pepper
2 onions
2 courgettes
3 × 15ml spoons/3 tablespoons olive oil
25g/1 oz butter
1 clove garlic
salt and pepper

GARNISH
2 large sprigs parsley

Skin the tomatoes and remove the pips. Chop coarsely (metal blade). Cut the aubergines into large pieces. Cut the pepper into large pieces. Cut the onions into pieces. Chop the aubergines, pepper and onions coarsely (metal blade). Slice the unpeeled courgettes (slicing disc). Put the oil and butter into a saucepan and heat together. Add all the vegetables. Crush the garlic and add with the salt and pepper. Stir well and cover tightly. Simmer for 1 hour until the vegetables are tender and the oil has been absorbed. Chop the parsley finely (metal blade) and sprinkle thickly on top. Serve hot or cold with crusty bread, or as an accompaniment to meat, fish or poultry.

COURGETTES IN TOMATO SAUCE

900g/2 lb courgettes
1 large onion
1 clove garlic
2 × 15ml spoons/2 tablespoons oil
450g/1 lb canned tomatoes
1 × 15ml spoon/1 tablespoon concentrated tomato purée
1 × 5ml spoon/1 teaspoon lemon juice
1 × 5ml spoon/1 teaspoon sugar
salt and pepper
50g/2 oz day-old white bread
25g/1 oz Cheddar cheese
a large sprig of parsley

Slice the unpeeled courgettes (slicing disc). Chop the onion and garlic finely (metal blade). Heat the oil in a pan and cook the onion and garlic over low heat, stirring well, for 5 minutes, until golden and soft. Stir in the tomatoes and their juice, the tomato purée, lemon juice, sugar, salt and pepper. Bring to the boil, then simmer and stir for 10 minutes. Stir in the sliced courgettes. Pour the mixture into a greased 1.2 litre/2 pint casserole. Discard the crusts and make the bread into crumbs (metal blade). Grate the cheese (grating disc). Chop the parsley (metal blade). Mix the crumbs, cheese and parsley and season lightly with salt and pepper. Sprinkle over the courgette mixture. Bake at 200°C/400°F/Gas 6 for 30 minutes. Serve as a dish on its own, or as an accompaniment to meat or fish.

SWEET AND SOUR RED CABBAGE

900g/2 lb red cabbage
2 small onions
1 eating apple
15g/½ oz butter
1 × 15ml spoon/1 tablespoon dark soft brown sugar
1 × 15ml spoon/1 tablespoon vinegar
300ml/½ pint dry cider
salt and pepper

Shred the cabbage (slicing disc). Chop the onions finely (metal blade). Peel and core the apple and chop coarsely (metal blade). Melt the butter in a pan and cook the onion for 5 minutes over low heat, stirring well. Add the sugar and vinegar and put in the cabbage. Stir well and add the cider, salt and pepper. Cover and simmer for 1 hour. Stir in the apple pieces and continue cooking for 1 hour.

Alternatively, cook the cabbage in the oven at 160°C/325°F/Gas 3 for 2 hours.

This recipe is particularly good with sausages, pork or duck.

AVOCADO SALAD

2 oranges
2 large sprigs parsley
3 × 15ml spoons/3 tablespoons oil
1 × 15ml spoon/1 tablespoon white wine vinegar
salt and pepper
2 avocado pears

Grate the rind from one orange, and squeeze out the juice. Peel the other orange and divide into segments, removing all the pith and skin. Mix the orange juice and rind, parsley, oil, vinegar, salt and pepper to a smooth dressing (plastic blade). Cut the avocado pears in half lengthways, remove the stones, and scoop out the flesh. Cut the flesh into small pieces and mix with the orange segments. Use to fill the avocado skins and pour over the dressing. Serve at once.

CUCUMBER SALAD

1 cucumber
salt and pepper
1 × 5ml spoon/1 teaspoon sugar
150ml/¼ pint white vinegar
150ml/¼ pint water
150ml/¼ pint natural yoghurt

GARNISH
2 large sprigs parsley

Peel the cucumber and slice (slicing disc). Sprinkle the slices with salt and leave for 30 minutes. Rinse and drain thoroughly. Mix the sugar with the vinegar and water and a shake of pepper. Pour over the cucumber and leave to stand in a refrigerator for 1 hour. Drain off the liquid and toss the cucumber in yoghurt. Chop the parsley finely (metal blade) and sprinkle on top. Serve chilled.

HEALTH SALAD

2 red-skinned eating apples
2 sticks celery
1 carrot
juice of ½ lemon
50g/2 oz peanuts
50g/2 oz seedless raisins
4 × 15ml spoons/4 tablespoons mayonnaise

GARNISH
watercress sprigs

Wipe but do not peel the apples. Cut them in quarters and remove the cores. Chop coarsley (metal blade). Slice the celery thinly (slicing disc). Grate the carrot, (grating disc), then mix with the apples and celery. Sprinkle the lemon juice over the salad so that the apples do not discolour. Chop the peanuts coarsely (metal blade), then add to the salad with the raisins. Toss in the mayonnaise and garnish with watercress sprigs.

JELLIED BEETROOT SALAD

4 beetroot
1 small onion
1 raspberry jelly tablet
300ml/½ pint white vinegar
300ml/½ pint water

Cook the beetroot, cool and rub off the skins. Chop coarsely (metal blade). Chop the onion finely (metal blade). Mix the beetroot and onion together in a bowl. Melt the jelly tablet in boiling vinegar and water and pour over the beetroot. Leave until set and then break up lightly with a fork.

FRESH SPINACH SALAD WITH BACON DRESSING

900g/2 lb spinach
8 rashers streaky bacon, without rinds
100g/4 oz day-old white bread
1 clove garlic
6 × 15ml spoons/6 tablespoons oil
3 × 15ml spoons/3 tablespoons lemon juice
½ × 2.5ml spoon/¼ teaspoon French mustard
salt and pepper

Chop the spinach coarsely (metal blade) and put into a salad bowl. Chop the bacon coarsely (metal blade). Put into a saucepan and heat until the fat runs. Let the bacon cook until crisp, then lift it from the fat with a perforated spoon and add to the spinach. Discard the crusts and break the bread into pieces. Process (metal blade) until just broken into small pieces but not crumbs. Crush the garlic. Toss the bread and garlic in the bacon fat until the pieces of bread are crisp and golden. Put the oil, lemon juice, mustard, salt and pepper into the processor bowl and mix thoroughly (plastic blade). Drain the bread pieces and garlic and add to the salad bowl. Pour on the dressing, toss quickly and serve at once.

CABBAGE AND CARROT COLESLAW

450g/1 lb firm white cabbage
½ small onion
2 celery sticks
2 carrots
1 eating apple
50g/2 oz walnut halves
4 × 15ml spoons/4 tablespoons mayonnaise
2 × 15ml spoons/2 tablespoons single cream
1 × 15ml spoon/1 tablespoon vinegar
a pinch of mustard powder

Shred the cabbage, slice the onion and celery (slicing disc). Grate the carrots (grating disc). Grate the apple (grating disc). Put all the prepared vegetables into a bowl. Chop the walnuts (metal blade). Add the apple and nuts to the vegetables. Stir together the mayonnaise, cream, vinegar and mustard. Pour over the other ingredients and toss well so that the dressing is mixed right through the salad.

Cabbage and Carrot Coleslaw

WALDORF SALAD

4 red-skinned eating apples
2 × 5ml spoons/2 teaspoons lemon juice
½ cucumber
3 celery sticks
75g/3 oz walnut halves
2 sprigs parsley
150ml/¼ pint mayonnaise
crisp lettuce leaves

GARNISH
watercress sprigs

Wipe and core the apples but do not peel them. Cut into quarters and chop coarsely (metal blade). Put into a bowl and sprinkle with lemon juice. Peel the cucumber and chop coarsely (metal blade). Chop the celery coarsely with the walnuts (metal blade). Mix the cucumber, celery and walnuts with the apples. Chop the parsley (metal blade) and add to the mixture. Stir in the mayonnaise until the pieces are well coated. Arrange the lettuce leaves on a serving dish and pile the salad in the centre. Garnish with watercress sprigs.

HOT CABBAGE SALAD

1 small white cabbage
2 egg yolks
15g/½ oz softened butter
2 × 15ml spoons/2 tablespoons cold water
2 × 15ml spoons/2 tablespoons hot vinegar
salt and pepper

Use a cabbage which is very crisp and firm. Cut into wedges, then shred (slicing disc) and put into a bowl of ice-chilled water for 30 minutes. Drain well and pat dry with kitchen paper. Mix the egg yolks lightly (plastic blade). With the machine running, add the other ingredients through the feeder tube until well blended. Put the mixture into a bowl over hot water or the top of a double saucepan. Stir constantly until creamy. Put the cabbage into a pan and pour over the sauce. Heat through and serve hot with cold meat.

BLUE CHEESE SALAD DRESSING

50g/2 oz Danish blue cheese
100g/4 oz cottage cheese
3 × 15ml spoons/3 tablespoons mayonnaise
2 × 15ml spoons/2 tablespoons single cream
1 × 5ml spoon/1 teaspoon French mustard
2 × 5ml spoons/2 teaspoons lemon juice
1 × 5ml spoon/1 teaspoon chopped chives

Chop the blue cheese in small pieces (metal blade). Add the other ingredients and process until smooth (plastic blade). Chill and serve on a green salad.

MAYONNAISE

1 egg and 1 egg yolk
1 × 2.5ml spoon/½ teaspoon mustard powder
salt and white pepper
300ml/½ pint salad oil
1 × 15ml spoon/1 tablespoon wine vinegar or lemon
juice

Mix the egg, egg yolk, mustard, salt and pepper until smooth (metal blade). With the machine running, pour half the oil slowly through the feeder tube (metal blade). Switch off the machine to change blades. Add the remaining oil through the feeder tube and mix until the mayonnaise is thick (plastic blade). Add vinegar or lemon juice and process until mixed.

Green Mayonnaise
Add 1 chopped garlic clove and 1 × 15ml spoon/1 tablespoon each finely chopped parsley, chives and basil to the mayonnaise. Process just long enough to blend.

Curry Mayonnaise
Add 1 × 15ml spoon/1 tablespoon concentrated tomato purée, 1 × 15ml spoon/1 tablespoon curry paste, 1 × 15ml spoon/1 teaspoon lemon juice and 2 × 15ml spoons/2 tablespoons double cream to the mayonnaise. Process just long enough to blend.

Nicoise Mayonnaise
Add 1 chopped garlic clove and 1 × 2.5ml spoon/½ teaspoon chopped tarragon with 2 × 15ml spoons/2 tablespoons concentrated tomato purée to the mayonnaise. Process to blend.

VINAIGRETTE SAUCE

4 × 15ml spoons/4 tablespoons oil
2 × 15ml spoons/2 tablespoons wine vinegar
1 × 2.5ml spoon/½ teaspoon salt
1 × 2.5ml spoon/½ teaspoon caster sugar
1 × 2.5ml spoon/½ teaspoon mustard powder
a pinch of pepper

Mix all the ingredients until well blended (plastic blade).
Use for green salads, tomatoes, cold leeks, asparagus, globe artichokes and avocado pears.

PUDDINGS, DESSERTS, ICES AND SWEET SAUCES

APPLE BATTER PUDDING

450g/1 lb eating apples
4 × 15ml spoons/4 tablespoons brandy **or** Calvados
a pinch of ground cinnamon
25g/1 oz butter
50g/2 oz light soft brown sugar

BATTER
3 eggs
150g/5 oz self-raising flour
4 × 15ml spoons/4 tablespoons milk

Peel and core the apples. Chop coarsely (metal blade). Put into a bowl with the brandy or Calvados and cinnamon and leave to stand for 1 hour. Use a little of the butter to grease an ovenproof dish. Put in the apples and brandy and sprinkle with the sugar. Dot with flakes of butter.

To make the batter, mix the eggs, flour and milk to a thick cream (plastic blade).

Pour the batter over the fruit and bake at 200°C/400°F/Gas 6 for 35 minutes until the batter is crisp and golden. Serve very hot with cream.

APRICOT CRUMBLE

450g/1 lb canned apricots
15g/½ oz butter
50g/2 oz light soft brown sugar
a pinch of ground cinnamon

TOPPING
50g/2 oz butter
25g/1 oz light soft brown sugar
75g/3 oz plain flour
a pinch of ground ginger

Drain the apricots and reserve the juice. Chop the fruit coarsely (metal blade). Put into a well greased ovenproof dish, dot with flakes of butter and sprinkle with sugar and cinnamon. Add 3 × 15ml spoons/3 tablespoons syrup from the can.

To make the topping, mix the butter, sugar, flour and ginger until the mixture is like coarse breadcrumbs (plastic blade). Sprinkle on top f the fruit and press down very lightly with a fork. Bake at 180°C/350°F/Gas 4 for 45 minutes.

Serve hot with cream or custard.

BISCUIT PUDDINGS

100g/4 oz digestive biscuits
100g/4 oz soft margarine
100g/4 oz dark soft brown sugar
150ml/¼ pint creamy milk
2 eggs and 2 egg yolks

Break the biscuits into pieces and make into coarse crumbs (metal blade). Put to one side. Cream the margarine and sugar (plastic blade). Add the biscuit crumbs, milk, egg and egg yolks. Process until well mixed. Put into 4–6 individual ovenproof dishes and bake at 180°C/350°F/Gas 4 for 25 minutes.

Serve with hot raspberry or apricot jam.

BLACKCURRANT CASTLES

100g/4 oz soft margarine
100g/4 oz caster sugar
2 eggs
100g/4 oz self-raising flour
½ × 2.5ml spoon/¼ teaspoon vanilla essence
2 × 15ml spoons/2 tablespoons warm water
4 × 5ml spoons/4 teaspoons blackcurrant jam

Mix the margarine, sugar, eggs, flour and essence to a soft consistency (plastic blade). With the motor running, add the water through the feeder tube until well mixed. Grease four castle pudding tins and place them on a baking sheet. Put a spoonful of jam in the base of each tin and cover with the sponge mixture. Bake at 180°C/350°F/Gas 4 for 25 minutes, then turn out and serve hot with some additional hot blackcurrant jam.

COFFEE WALNUT PUDDING AND COFFEE CREAM SAUCE

50g/2 oz walnut halves
100g/4 oz soft margarine
100g/4 oz caster sugar
2 eggs
175g/6 oz self-raising flour
2 × 5ml spoons/2 teaspoons coffee powder
1 × 15ml spoon/1 tablespoon milk

SAUCE
2 eggs
6 × 15ml spoons/6 tablespoons hot strong coffee
50g/2 oz caster sugar
a pinch of salt
150ml/¼ pint double cream

Chop the walnuts coarsely (metal blade) and put to one side. Cream the margarine and caster sugar until soft and fluffy (plastic blade). With the motor running, add the eggs, one at a time, with a little flour, through the feeder tube. When they are incorporated, switch off the machine. Add the flour, coffee powder and milk, and mix just long enough to make a soft dough. Stir in the walnuts. Put the mixture in a greased 900ml/1½ pint pudding basin. Cover with a piece of greased greaseproof paper, and cover again with foil. Put into a saucepan with boiling water to come half-way up the sides of the basin. Cover the pan with a lid and boil for 1½ hours, adding more boiling water from time to time so that the pan does not become dry.

Meanwhile, prepare the sauce. Beat the eggs lightly (plastic blade). With the motor running, pour the coffee, sugar and salt through the feeder tube until the mixture is well blended. Pour into the top of a double saucepan, or into a basin over hot water, and cook without boiling until the mixture is thick enough to coat the back of a spoon. Leave until cold. Whip the cream to soft peaks. Add the coffee mixture and continue whipping until just mixed.

Turn the pudding on to a warm serving plate and serve the cold sauce separately.

COLLEGE PUDDING AND BRANDY BUTTER

75g/3 oz day-old brown bread
50g/2 oz self-raising flour
50g/2 oz shredded suet
1 × 2.5ml spoon/½ teaspoon ground mixed spice
50g/2 oz light soft brown sugar
1 egg
4 × 15ml spoons/4 tablespoons milk
75g/3 oz mixed dried fruit
25g/1 oz chopped mixed candied peel

BRANDY BUTTER
100g/4 oz unsalted butter
grated rind of 1 lemon
100g/4 oz caster sugar
2 × 15ml spoons/2 tablespoons brandy

Discard the crusts and make the bread into crumbs (metal blade). Put to one side. Mix the flour, suet, spice, sugar, egg and milk to a soft dough (plastic blade). Add the crumbs and mix until just incorporated. Stir in the fruit and peel. Put the mixture in a greased 900ml/1½ pint pudding basin, cover with greased greaseproof paper, then cover again with foil. Put into a saucepan with boiling water to come half-way up the side of the basin. Cover the pan with a lid and boil for 2 hours, adding more boiling water from time to time so that the pan does not become dry.

To make the brandy butter, cream the butter with the grated lemon rind (plastic blade). With the motor running, add a little sugar and brandy alternatively until completely incorporated. Put into a serving dish and chill.

Turn out the pudding and serve with the chilled brandy butter.

DATE PUDDING

225g/8 oz day-old white bread
350g/12 oz stoned dates
15g/½ oz blanched almonds
100g/4 oz shredded suet
a pinch of salt
1 egg
2 × 15ml spoons/2 tablespoons golden syrup

Discard the crusts and make the bread into crumbs (metal blade). Put to one side. Cut the dates into chunks, chop coarsely (metal blade) and mix with the almonds. Mix the suet, breadcrumbs, salt, egg and syrup to a soft dough (plastic blade). Stir in the dates and almonds. Put the mixture in a greased 1.2 litre/2 pint pudding basin, cover with greased greaseproof paper, then cover again with foil. Put into a saucepan with boiling water to come half-way up the sides of the basin. Cover the pan with a lid and boil for 2 hours, adding more boiling water from time to time so that the pan does not become dry. Turn out and serve with warm golden syrup or marmalade.

GOLDEN PINEAPPLE SPONGE

25g/1 oz butter
2 × 15ml spoons/2 tablespoons dark soft brown sugar
450g/1 lb canned pineapple rings
6 glacé cherries
100g/4 oz soft margarine
100g/4 oz caster sugar
2 eggs
100g/4 oz self-raising flour

Grease a 1.2 litre/2 pint pie dish liberally with butter. Sprinkle with the brown sugar. Drain the pineapple rings and arrange six rings in the base of the pie dish. Place a cherry in the centre of each ring. Chop the remaining pineapple coarsely (metal blade) and put to one side. Mix the margarine and sugar with the eggs and flour until well creamed (plastic blade). Stir in the chopped pineapple and spread over the pineapple rings in the pie dish. Bake at 180°C/350°F/Gas 4 for 45 minutes. Turn out and serve with custard.

RHUBARB TOFFEE PUDDING

25g/1 oz butter
50g/2 oz light soft brown sugar
675g/1½ lb rhubarb
225g/8 oz self-raising flour
1 × 5ml spoon/1 teaspoon salt
75g/3 oz shredded suet
150ml/¼ pint cold water
100g/4 oz sugar
50g/2 oz sultanas
25g/1 oz chopped mixed candied peel
grated rind and juice of ½ lemon
a pinch of ground cinnamon
6 × 15ml spoons/6 tablespoons water

Grease a 1.2 litre/2 pint pudding basin liberally with the butter and sprinkle with the brown sugar. Cut the rhubarb in pieces and chop coarsely (metal blade). Mix the flour, salt, suet and cold water to a soft dough (plastic blade). Cut off one-third for a lid. Roll out the remaining dough very lightly and line the pudding basin. Put in half the rhubarb. In a bowl, mix the sugar, sultanas, peel, grated rind and juice of the lemon, and the cinnamon. Sprinkle this mixture on to the rhubarb and cover with the remaining rhubarb. Add the water. Cover with the remaining dough. Cover with a piece of greased greaseproof paper. Bake at 180°C/350°F/Gas 4 for 1¼ hours. Turn out and serve with cream or custard.

CHOCOLATE CHIFFON PIE

150g/5 oz plain chocolate digestive biscuits
100g/4 oz butter
100g/4 oz sugar

FILLING
300ml/½ pint whipping cream
2 × 5ml spoons/2 teaspoons gelatine
2 × 15ml spoons/2 tablespoons water
250ml/8 fl oz milk
50g/2 oz plain chocolate
3 eggs, separated
100g/4 oz sugar
a pinch of salt
3 drops vanilla essence

DECORATION (OPTIONAL)
plain chocolate, grated
whipped cream

Break the biscuits into pieces and make into crumbs (metal blade). Melt the butter in a pan and add the sugar and crumbs. Press into a greased 25cm/10 inch ovenproof dish and bake at 180°C/350°F/Gas 4 for 15 minutes. Cool at room temperature and then chill in a refrigerator until firm.

To make the filling, whip the cream to soft peaks and put to one side. Mix the gelatine and water in a small bowl or cup and stand the bowl in a pan of hot water until the gelatine melts and is syrupy. Heat the milk and chocolate together until just below boiling point. Mix the egg yolks (plastic blade). Start the machine, pour in the sugar, salt and essence through the feeder tube, and gradually pour in the milk mixture. When the eggs and milk are combined, return to the saucepan and cook very gently until the mixture thickens like custard. Remove from the heat and cool for 10 minutes, then stir in the gelatine. Leave until thick and cool. Mix with the cream just long enough to blend together (plastic blade), then turn into another bowl. Whisk the egg whites to stiff peaks. Fold into the cream mixture and pour on to the biscuit base. Chill before serving. If liked, decorate with whirls of whipped cream and grated chocolate.

CREAM CHEESE AND APPLE FLAN

225g/8 oz prepared shortcrust pastry (page 75)
450g/1 lb eating apples
50g/2 oz light soft brown sugar
1 × 15ml spoon/1 tablespoon orange marmalade
1 × 2.5ml spoon/½ teaspoon ground mixed spice
100g/4 oz soft cream cheese
150ml/¼ pint double cream

Line a 20cm/8 inch flan tin with the pastry, and bake blind at 200°C/400°F/Gas 6 for 25 minutes. Cool and put on to a serving dish. Peel and core the apples. Chop coarsely (metal blade). Put into a pan with the sugar, marmalade and spice, and simmer gently until the apples are soft. Cool for 10 minutes, then return to the processor bowl and mix until smooth (plastic blade). Leave until completely cold. Spread the flan case with the cream cheese and place the apple purée on top. Whip the cream to soft peaks and spoon on top of the apples. Chill for 1 hour before serving.

Chocolate Chiffon Pie

FRESH FRUIT FOOL

225g/8 oz fresh raspberries, strawberries **or** blackberries
75g/3 oz caster sugar
grated rind of ½ orange
1 × 5ml spoon/1 teaspoon lemon juice
150ml/¼ pint double cream

DECORATION
whipped cream
raspberries, strawberries **or** blackberries

Mix the berries to a purée with the sugar, orange rind and lemon juice (metal blade). Put the purée through a sieve to get rid of any pips. Whip the cream to soft peaks and put into the processor. With the machine running, pour in the fruit purée through the feeder tube until the cream and fruit are just mixed. Spoon into tall glasses and chill for 1 hour before serving. Decorate with a whirl of whipped cream topped with a piece of fresh fruit.

FUDGE PIE

150g/5 oz plain chocolate digestive biscuits
100g/4 oz butter
100g/4 oz sugar

FILLING
100g/4 oz walnut halves
100g/4 oz marshmallows
225g/8 oz butter
150g/5 oz caster sugar
50g/2 oz plain chocolate
1 × 2.5ml spoon/½ teaspoon vanilla essence
2 eggs

Break the biscuits into pieces and make into crumbs (metal blade). Melt the butter in a pan and add the sugar and crumbs. Press into a greased 25cm/10 inch pie plate and bake at 180°C/ 350°F/Gas 4 for 15 minutes. Cool at room temperature and then chill in a refrigerator until firm.

To make the filling, chop the walnuts coarsely (metal blade). Chop the marshmallows into small pieces (metal blade). Cream the butter and sugar until light and fluffy (plastic blade). Melt the chocolate with the essence in a pan and add to the creamed mixture with the eggs. Continue processing until creamy. Fold in the nuts and marshmallows and put into the crumb case. Chill for 2 hours before serving.

OLD ENGLISH CHEESECAKE

225g/8 oz prepared shortcrust pastry (page 75)
50g/2 oz butter
350g/12 oz soft curd cheese
75g/3 oz caster sugar
2 eggs
1 × 15ml spoon/1 tablespoon brandy
2 × 15ml spoons/2 tablespoons single cream
a pinch of ground mixed spice
50g/2 oz seedless raisins

Line a 20cm/8 inch flan tin with the pastry and bake blind at 200°C/400°F/Gas 6 for 25 minutes. Leave to cool. Cut the butter into pieces and mix with the curd cheese, sugar, eggs, brandy, cream and spice until smooth (plastic blade). Stir in the raisins and put into the pastry case. Bake at 160°C/325°F/Gas 3 for 40 minutes. Serve cold.

VICTORIAN CHOCOLATE SHAPE

450g/1 lb day-old white bread
600ml/1 pint milk
50g/2 oz dark soft brown sugar
50g/2 oz plain chocolate

Discard the crusts and make the bread into crumbs (metal blade). Put into a bowl with the milk and sugar and leave to soak for 15 minutes. Grate the chocolate (grating disc) and stir into the mixture. Put the mixture into a greased 1.2 litre/2 pint pudding basin and cover with a piece of greased greaseproof paper. Cover again with foil. Put into a saucepan with boiling water to come half-way up the sides of the basin. Cover the pan with a lid and boil for 2 hours, adding more boiling water from time to time so that the pan does not become dry. Leave until cold before turning out.

Serve with custard or chocolate sauce (see Profiteroles, page 56) or with ice cream.

PEACH SHORTCAKE

225g/8 oz self-raising flour
1 × 2.5ml spoon/½ teaspoon salt
a pinch of ground nutmeg
25g/1 oz caster sugar
50g/2 oz soft margarine
150ml/¼ pint milk

FILLING AND TOPPING
50g/2 oz softened butter
450g/1 lb canned peach slices
150ml/¼ pint double cream

Put the flour, salt, nutmeg and sugar into the processor bowl and add the margarine. Pour in the milk and mix to a soft dough (plastic blade). Divide the dough into two pieces and roll out lightly to fit a 20cm/8 inch greased sandwich tin. Put in one piece of dough and brush lightly with a little of the softened butter. Put the other piece of dough on top. Bake at 230°C/450°F/Gas 8 for 12 minutes. Turn on to a wire rack. Carefully split the layers and put the bottom half on to a serving plate.

Spread each half with the softened butter. Drain the peach halves and arrange two-thirds of them on the bottom layer. Top with the second layer. Whip the cream to soft peaks and spoon over the top of the shortcake. Decorate with the remaining peach slices. Serve while freshly baked.

PROFITEROLES WITH CHOCOLATE SAUCE

½ quantity of choux pastry (page 74)
150ml/¼ pint double cream

SAUCE
100g/4 oz plain chocolate
225g/8 oz sugar
150ml/¼ pint hot coffee
a pinch of salt
1 × 2.5ml spoon/½ teaspoon vanilla essence

Put teaspoons of the choux pastry on a lightly greased baking sheet, and bake at 200°C/400°F/Gas 6 for 20 minutes. Cool on a wire rack. Whip the cream to soft peaks and use to fill the profiteroles. Pile into a serving dish.

To make the sauce, chop the chocolate finely (metal blade). Blend all the sauce ingredients in small quantities until smooth (plastic blade). Serve the sauce hot or cold over the profiteroles.

Note The sauce may be made in advance and stored in a covered jar in a refrigerator.

BROWN BREAD ICE CREAM AND APRICOT SAUCE

100g/4 oz day-old brown bread
300ml/½ pint double cream
150ml/¼ pint single cream
75g/3 oz icing sugar
1 × 15ml spoon/1 tablespoon rum
2 eggs, separated

APRICOT SAUCE
450g/1 lb canned apricots
4 × 15ml spoons/4 tablespoons dark chunky marmalade

Discard the crusts and make the bread into crumbs (metal blade). Spread the crumbs on a baking sheet, and bake at 150°C/300°F/Gas 2 for 10 minutes. Leave until cold. Whip the double cream until just stiff and gradually pour in the single cream, whipping to soft peaks. Put into the processor. Add the icing sugar, rum and egg yolks, and mix for 10 seconds (plastic blade). Add the crumbs and mix for 5 seconds. Whisk the egg whites to soft peaks and fold into the mixture. Pour into a freezer tray and freeze at the lowest setting for 3 hours. This ice cream does not need beating while freezing.

To prepare the sauce, blend the apricots and their syrup with the marmalade until smooth (metal blade). Chill the sauce while the ice cream is freezing.

Spoon the ice cream into glasses and serve with the sauce.

Brown Bread Ice Cream and Apricot Sauce

BASIC ICE CREAM

450ml/¾ pint milk
1 vanilla pod
2 size 1–2 egg yolks
50g/2 oz caster sugar
a pinch of salt
150ml/¼ pint double cream

Warm the milk with the vanilla pod just to boiling point. Remove the vanilla pod. Cool the milk slightly and then thoroughly blend with the egg yolks, sugar and salt (plastic blade). Cook in a double saucepan (or in a bowl over hot water) until the mixture is of a coating consistency. Leave to cool. Whip the cream lightly and fold into the custard. Pour into a freezer tray and freeze at the lowest setting for 1 hour, then scoop out the half-frozen mixture into the processor, and mix until smooth (metal blade). Return to the freezer tray and freeze for 1 hour. Scoop out again and mix in the processor until smooth. Return to the freezer tray and freeze for 1 hour.

Variations
1) Melt 50g/2 oz plain chocolate in 4 × 15ml spoons/4 table-spoons hot water, and add to the vanilla-flavoured milk before mixing with the egg yolks.
2) Omit the vanilla. Add 1 × 15ml spoon/1 tablespoon instant coffee powder to the milk as it is heated before mixing with the eggs.
3) Add 75g/3oz mixed dried fruit, 25g/1oz chopped mixed candied peel and 25g/1 oz chopped nuts to the vanilla ice before freezing.

FROZEN ORANGE PUDDING

12 macaroons
juice of 1 orange
juice of 1 lemon
3 eggs, separated
100g/4 oz sugar
a pinch of salt
300ml/½ pint double cream

Break the macaroons into pieces and make into coarse crumbs (metal blade). Sprinkle half the crumbs in an ice-making tray and reserve the rest. Beat the juices, egg yolks, sugar and salt until well mixed (plastic blade). Pour into the top of a double saucepan or a bowl over boiling water, and cook until thick and creamy. Leave until cool.

Whip the cream to soft peaks. Whisk the egg whites to stiff peaks. Fold the cream and then the egg whites into the cooled orange mixture. Pour on top of the macaroon crumbs, and top with the remaining crumbs. Freeze in the ice-making compartment of a refrigerator at lowest setting for 4 hours, then transfer to the main part of the refrigerator for 1 hour before serving. Turn on to a serving dish and cut into thick slices.

Quick Fruit Ice Cream

300g/10oz prepared fruit (see **Note**)
100g/4oz caster sugar
150ml/¼pint double cream

Weigh the fruit after removing skins and stones where necessary. Cut into pieces and mix with the sugar until the fruit is finely chopped (metal blade). Add the cream and continue mixing until smooth. Pour into a freezing tray and freeze at the lowest setting for 2–3 hours until firm.

Note Suitable fruit for this ice cream are strawberries, raspberries, blackcurrants, apricots, peaches, bananas, cherries or pineapple.

Custard Sauce

1 egg
50g/2oz caster sugar
25g/1oz butter
1 × 2.5ml spoon/½ teaspoon vanilla essence
600ml/1 pint milk
25g/1oz cornflour

Mix the egg, sugar, butter and essence until creamy (plastic blade). Mix 3 × 15ml spoons/3 tablespoons milk with the cornflour. Bring the rest of the milk to the boil. Pour on to the cornflour and return to the pan. Cook for 2 minutes over low heat, stirring all the time. With the machine running, pour the milk mixture slowly through the feeder tube and continue processing until smooth. Serve hot or cold.

Confectioner's Custard

2 egg yolks
50g/2oz sugar
25g/1oz plain flour
300ml/½pint milk
15g/½oz unsalted butter
a few drops vanilla essence

Mix the egg yolks, sugar, flour and half the milk until smooth (plastic blade). With the machine running, add the remaining milk through the feeder tube until blended. Put into a saucepan and cook gently over low heat, stirring well until thick. Remove from the heat, add the butter and essence, and cool.
Use for filling cakes, choux buns or the base of fruit flans.

Variations
For a lighter filling, mix the cold custard with an equal quantity of softly whipped double cream. The custard may be flavoured with a liqueur or a little coffee essence.

Rum Butter

225g/8oz unsalted butter
225g/8oz light soft brown sugar
6 × 15ml spoons/6 tablespoons light rum

Cut the butter into small pieces and process until soft (plastic blade). Add half the sugar and process until light and fluffy. With the machine running, add the remaining sugar and the rum in small amounts through the feeder tube until well mixed. This must be done slowly or the mixture may curdle. Put into a serving dish and chill.
Serve with puddings or mince pies, or as a spread on biscuits.

Breads, Cakes, Biscuits, Icings and Pastry

Basic White Bread

7g/¼ oz fresh yeast **or** 1 × 5ml spoon/1 teaspoon dried
yeast
150ml/¼ pint warm water
225g/8 oz strong plain flour
1 × 5ml spoon/1 teaspoon salt
15g/½ oz lard
poppy, caraway **or** sesame seeds (optional)

Blend the fresh yeast in the warm water or reconstitute the dried yeast. Mix the flour, salt and lard (plastic blade). Add the yeast liquid and mix for 1 minute. Yeast may also be added through the feeder tube, with the machine running. Flour your hands lightly and shape the dough into a ball. Leave in a greased polythene bag in a warm place for about 1 hour until the dough has doubled in size. Return to the processor bowl and mix for 1 minute (plastic blade). Shape the dough into the required shape and return to the greased polythene bag. Leave to prove for 40 minutes. Remove from the bag. Sprinkle with poppy, caraway or sesame seeds, if liked, and bake at 220°C/425°F/Gas 7 for 30 minutes. Cool on a wire rack.

Variation

Brown Bread
Substitute wholemeal flour for half the white flour.

To shape bread

Plait
After the dough has risen, divide into three pieces. Lightly roll with the hands on a floured surface to form three cylinders about 30cm/12 inches long. Pinch the ends of these cylinders together at one end and plait them together. Pinch the other ends after plaiting. Tuck the ends underneath to keep them firm and give a rounded end to the plait. The dough is now ready for proving.

Crown
After the dough has risen, divide it into seven pieces, kneading each one into a ball. Grease a 20cm/8 inch sandwich tin and arrange six balls around the edge. Place the last ball in the centre. After proving, the balls will have joined together to form a 'crown'. This is a useful shape for serving as each person has one section of the loaf, which is like an individual roll.

Dinner Rolls
After the dough has risen, divide into eight pieces, kneading each one into a ball. Grease a baking sheet and place the dough on it. Prove as for loaves. Bake at 220°C/425°F/Gas 7 for 15 minutes.

Muffins
Make up the recipe with white flour. After the dough has risen, roll out on a floured surface 1cm/½ inch thick. Leave to rest for 5 minutes covered with polythene, and cut out 9cm/3½ inch rounds. Place on a well floured baking sheet and dust the tops with flour or fine semolina. Oil a polythene bag and put the dough in it. Leave for 40 minutes in a warm place. Cook on a hot greased griddle or heavy-based frying pan for 6 minutes each side until golden-brown. Alternatively, bake at 230°C/450°F/Gas 8 for 10 minutes, turning the muffins over after 5 minutes.

To serve, pull the muffins open all the way round with the fingers, leaving the halves joined in the middle. Toast slowly on both sides. Pull apart, butter each half well, put together again and serve hot.

A selection of white breads

MINCEMEAT DOUGHNUTS

15g/½ oz fresh yeast **or** 7g/¼ oz dried yeast
150ml/¼ pint cider
25g/1 oz block margarine
225g/8 oz strong plain flour
a pinch of salt
2 × 15ml spoons/2 tablespoons fruit mincemeat
fat **or** oil for deep frying
100g/4 oz caster sugar
1 × 2.5ml spoon/½ teaspoon ground cinnamon

Heat the cider to lukewarm. Blend in the fresh yeast or reconstitute the dried yeast. Leave in a warm place for 10 minutes until the liquid is frothy. Cut the margarine into pieces and mix with the flour and salt just long enough to break up the margarine and mix with the flour (plastic blade). With the machine running, pour the yeast liquid through the feeder tube and mix to a soft dough. Flour your hands and shape the dough into a ball. Leave in a greased polythene bag in a warm place for about 45 minutes until the dough has doubled in size. Divide the dough into 12 pieces and knead each one lightly into a ball. Make a deep hole in each and put 1 × 2.5ml spoon/½ teaspoon mincemeat in each hole. Mould the dough round so that the mincemeat is covered. Put the dough balls on a greased baking sheet and return to the polythene bag. Leave in a warm place for 15 minutes. Remove from the bag. Fry the doughnuts in hot deep fat or oil for 10 minutes, turning occasionally until golden-brown. Drain on kitchen paper. Mix the sugar and cinnamon, and roll the hot doughnuts in this mixture until completely coated. Eat while fresh.

STICKY MALT LOAF

15g/½ oz fresh yeast **or** 7g/¼ oz dried yeast
125ml/4 fl oz warm water
225g/8 oz strong plain flour
a pinch of salt
3 × 15ml spoons/3 tablespoons malt extract
1 × 15ml spoon/1 tablespoon black treacle
25g/1 oz butter
100g/4 oz sultanas
1 × 15ml spoon/1 tablespoon clear honey

Blend the fresh yeast in the warm water or reconstitute the dried yeast. Leave in a warm place for 10 minutes until the liquid is frothy. Put the flour and salt into the processor bowl. Heat together the malt extract, treacle and butter until the fat has just melted. With the machine running, pour the yeast liquid through the feeder tube and then the malt liquid and process to a soft dough (plastic blade). Stir in the dried fruit. Flour your hands and shape the dough into a ball. Leave in a greased polythene bag for 45 minutes in a warm place until doubled in size. Knead lightly and shape into a cylinder. Put into a greased 450g/1 lb loaf tin and return to the greased bag and leave until the dough reaches the top of the tin. Remove the bag and bake at 200°C/400°F/Gas 6 for 45 minutes. Turn on to a wire rack and brush all over with a wet pastry brush dipped in honey. Leave until cold. Serve sliced and buttered.

RICH FRUIT BUNS

5 × 15ml spoons/5 tablespoons milk
7g/¼ oz fresh yeast **or** 1 × 5ml spoon/1 teaspoon dried yeast
225g/8 oz strong plain flour
a pinch of salt
a pinch of ground mixed spice
25g/1 oz butter
1 egg
75g/3 oz mixed dried fruit

GLAZE
25g/1 oz sugar
4 × 15ml spoons/4 tablespoons water

Heat the milk to lukewarm and blend in the fresh yeast or reconstitute the dried yeast. Leave in a warm place for 10 minutes until the liquid is frothy. Put the flour, salt, spice and remaining sugar into the processor bowl. Cut the butter into pieces and add to the bowl. Process until just mixed (plastic blade). With the machine running, pour the yeast liquid through the feeder tube and process to a soft dough. Add the egg and process until just mixed. Stir in the dried fruit. Flour your hands and shape the dough into a ball. Leave in a greased polythene bag in a warm place for about 1 hour until the dough has doubled in size. Divide into 10 pieces and knead each one lightly into a ball. Place the dough balls on a greased baking sheet, and return to the oiled bag. Leave in a warm place for 15 minutes. Remove the bag and bake the buns at 220°C/425°F/Gas 7 for 15 minutes. Put on to a wire rack.

For the glaze, put the sugar and water into a small pan, stir until dissolved and boil for 3 minutes. Brush the glaze on to the hot buns.

HOT CHEESE LOAVES

50g/2 oz Cheddar cheese
225g/8 oz plain flour
1½ × 5ml spoons/1½ teaspoons baking powder
½ × 2.5ml spoon/¼ teaspoon salt
50g/2 oz block margarine
6 × 15ml spoons/6 tablespoons milk
a pinch of dried mixed herbs

Grate the cheese (grating disc) and put to one side. Put the flour, baking powder and salt into the processor bowl. Cut the margarine into small pieces and add to the bowl. Process until the mixture is like coarse breadcrumbs (plastic blade). With the machine running, pour the milk gradually through the feeder tube and mix to a soft dough. Add the herbs and cheese and mix until just blended. Form the dough into two round cakes and place on a greased baking sheet. Flatten slightly and mark each circle deeply in a cross with a knife. Bake at 230°C/450°F/Gas 8 for 15 minutes. Cut each circle into four wedges. Split each one through, spread with butter and serve hot.

Note This cheese bread makes a good accompaniment to a salad meal.

PEANUT BUTTER LOAF

50g/2 oz salted peanuts
100g/4 oz light soft brown sugar
75g/3 oz peanut butter
225g/8 oz self-raising flour
a pinch of salt
1 size 7 egg
150ml/¼ pint milk

Chop the peanuts coarsely (metal blade) and put to one side. Cream the sugar and peanut butter until light and fluffy (plastic blade). Add the flour and salt, and mix until just blended. With the machine running, gradually add the egg and milk through the feeder tube, and mix to a soft dough. Stir in the peanuts. Put the mixture in a greased 450g/1 lb loaf tin and bake at 190°C/375°F/Gas 5 for 45 minutes. Turn out and cool on a wire rack. Serve sliced and buttered.

DORSET APPLE CAKE

225g/8 oz eating apples
100g/4 oz butter
100g/4 oz sugar
1 egg
225g/8 oz plain flour
1½ × 5ml spoons/1½ teaspoons baking powder
a pinch of salt

FILLING AND TOPPING
75g/3 oz butter
75g/3 oz light soft brown sugar

DECORATION
blanched almonds

Peel and core the apples. Cut them into quarters and then chop coarsely (metal blade). Put to one side. Cream the butter and sugar until light and fluffy (plastic blade). Add the egg, and cream the mixture for 10 seconds. Sift together the flour, baking powder and salt. Add to the creamed mixture and mix for a few seconds until incorporated. Stir in the chopped apple. Put the mixture in a greased 20cm/8 inch round cake tin, and bake at 180°C/350°F/Gas 4 for 50 minutes. Cool on a wire rack. After 10 minutes, split through the cake with a sharp knife.

To make the filling, cream the butter and brown sugar until light and fluffy (plastic blade). Sprinkle half the mixture between the pieces of cake, and use the rest to spread on top. Decorate with almonds. Eat freshly baked.

Dorset Apple Cake

TREACLE RAISIN LOAF

25g/1 oz mixed nuts
100g/4 oz plain flour
100g/4 oz plain wholemeal flour
50g/2 oz granulated sugar
75g/3 oz black treacle
150ml/¼ pint milk
1 × 5ml spoon/1 teaspoon bicarbonate of soda
1 size 7 egg
75g/3 oz seedless raisins

Chop the nuts finely (metal blade). Put the flours and sugar into the processor bowl. Heat together the black treacle and milk until lukewarm. Stir in the bicarbonate of soda. With the machine running, pour the mixture through the feeder tube until well blended (plastic blade). Add the egg and mix to a firm dough. Stir in the chopped nuts and the raisins. Put the mixture in a greased 450g/1 lb loaf tin, and bake at 180°C/350°F/Gas 4 for 1 hour. Cool on a wire rack. Serve sliced and buttered.

BASIC SANDWICH CAKE

175g/6 oz self-raising flour
1½ × 5ml spoons/1½ teaspoons baking powder
175g/6 oz soft margarine
175g/6 oz caster sugar
3 eggs

Sift the flour and baking powder into the processor bowl. Add the remaining ingredients and mix until light and fluffy (plastic blade). Divide the mixture between two 17.5cm/7 inch sandwich tins, and bake at 180°C/350°F/Gas 4 for 30 minutes. Cool on a wire rack.

Variations

Chocolate Sandwich
Add 25g/1 oz cocoa and 1 × 15ml spoon/1 tablespoon milk to the ingredients. Finish with chocolate butter cream for the filling and topping, and sprinkle with 50g/2 oz chopped walnuts.

Coffee Sandwich
Add 1 × 15ml spoon/1 tablespoon coffee essence to the ingredients. Finish with coffee butter cream for the filling and topping.

Cream Sandwich
Whip 150ml/¼ pint double cream to soft peaks. Spread a little jam on one cake, top with cream and put on the second cake. Sprinkle the top with caster or icing sugar. Chopped fresh, canned or frozen fruit may be mixed with the cream.

Jam Sandwich
Sandwich the cakes together with jam and sprinkle the top with caster sugar or sifted icing sugar.

Lemon or Orange Sandwich
Add 1 × 5ml spoon/1 teaspoon grated lemon or orange rind and 1 × 15ml spoon/1 tablespoon lemon or orange juice to the ingredients. Finish with the appropriate cream for the filling and topping.

APRICOT SPICE CAKE

100g/4oz soft margarine
175g/6oz caster sugar
2 eggs
4 × 15ml spoons/4 tablespoons hot water
300g/10oz plain flour
1 × 5ml spoon/1 teaspoon bicarbonate of soda
1 × 5ml spoon/1 teaspoon ground mixed spice
225g/8oz apricot jam

ICING (OPTIONAL)
100g/4oz icing sugar
2 × 15ml spoons/2 tablespoons orange juice

Mix the margarine and sugar until light and fluffy (plastic blade). With the machine running, add the eggs, one at a time through the feeder tube, and then the hot water. Sift together the flour, bicarbonate of soda and spice. Add to the mixture with the apricot jam, and process until completely blended. Put the mixture in a greased 20cm/8 inch round cake tin, and bake at 180°C/350°F/Gas 4 for 1¼ hours. Cool on a wire rack.

The cake may be finished with icing. Stir together the icing sugar and orange juice and spread over the cake.

TRUFFLE CAKES

225g/8oz any stale cake
25g/1oz cocoa
1 × 15ml spoon/1 tablespoon rum **or** brandy
150ml/¼ pint syrup from canned fruit **or** diluted orange squash
4 × 15ml spoons/4 tablespoons apricot jam
3 × 15ml spoons/3 tablespoons water
100g/4oz chocolate vermicelli
a little icing sugar

Break the cake into pieces and make into crumbs (metal blade). Change to the plastic blade and add the cocoa and rum or brandy. With the machine running, add the syrup or squash slowly through the feeder tube (plastic blade). The mixture should be firm enough to roll easily in the hands, so check the consistency before adding all the liquid, and omit a little if necessary. Roll the mixture with the hands into 12 balls. Leave in a refrigerator for 1 hour.

Heat together the apricot jam and water in a small pan until the jam has melted. Put the chocolate vermicelli on a plate. Using tongs or two spoons, dip the chilled truffle balls quickly in the jam and roll in the vermicelli. Put into paper cake cases. Leave for 1 hour until firm, and sprinkle the tops lightly with a little sifted icing sugar.

WALNUT GINGERBREAD

75g/3 oz walnut halves
25g/1 oz crystallized ginger
50g/2 oz soft margarine
50g/2 oz light soft brown sugar
225g/8 oz self-raising flour
2 × 5ml spoons/2 teaspoons ground ginger
1 × 5ml spoon/1 teaspoon baking powder
½ × 2.5ml spoon/¼ teaspoon salt
1 egg
150ml/¼ pint milk
2 × 5ml spoons/2 teaspoons Demerara sugar

Chop the walnuts and crystallized ginger finely (metal blade). Put to one side. Cream together the margarine and sugar (plastic blade). Add the flour, ground ginger, baking powder, salt, egg and milk, and mix to a very soft dough. Add the chopped walnuts and crystallized ginger and mix until blended. Put the mixture in a greased 450g/1 lb loaf tin and sprinkle with Demerara sugar. Bake at 180°C/350°F/Gas 4 for 1 hour 5 minutes. Cool on a wire rack. Serve sliced and buttered.

CHOCOLATE CHIP ORANGE CAKES

50g/2 oz plain chocolate
50g/2 oz soft margarine
50g/2 oz caster sugar
1 egg
75g/3 oz self-raising flour
grated rind and juice of 1 orange

Chop the chocolate finely (metal blade). Mix the margarine, sugar, egg and flour with the orange rind and juice until light and soft (plastic blade). Stir in the chocolate pieces. Put into 12 paper cases on a baking sheet and bake at 190°C/375°F/Gas 5 for 15 minutes. Cool on a wire rack.

DATE AND WALNUT CAKE

50g/2 oz walnut halves
225g/8 oz stoned dates
175g/6 oz soft margarine
175g/6 oz light soft brown sugar
225g/8 oz plain flour
1½ × 5ml spoons/1½ teaspoons baking powder
3 eggs
2 × 15ml spoons/2 tablespoons milk
3 × 15ml spoons/3 tablespoons icing sugar

Chop the walnuts coarsely (metal blade). Chop the dates finely (metal blade). Put the dates and walnuts to one side. Cream the margarine and sugar until light and fluffy (plastic blade). Sift together the flour and baking powder. Add the eggs, one at a time, with a little of the flour and milk through the feeder tube, mixing for 10 seconds after each addition. Add the remaining flour and mix just long enough for the flour to be incorporated. Stir in the dates and nuts. Put the mixture in a 900g/2 lb greased loaf tin, and bake at 160°C/325°F/Gas 3 for 1½ hours. Cool in the tin for 10 minutes, then turn out on to a wire rack to finish cooling. Sift the icing sugar over the top just before serving.

Date and Walnut Cake

HONEY CHEESECAKE

225g/8 oz prepared shortcrust pastry (page 75)
100g/4 oz cottage cheese
50g/2 oz honey
50g/2 oz caster sugar
25g/1 oz butter
2 eggs
1 × 2.5ml spoon/½ teaspoon ground cinnamon

TOPPING
25g/1 oz caster sugar
1 × 2.5ml spoon/½ teaspoon ground cinnamon

Roll out the pastry and use to line a 20cm/8 inch pie plate. Blend the cottage cheese, honey, sugar, butter, eggs and cinnamon until smooth (plastic blade). Put into the pastry case and sprinkle with a topping made of caster sugar and cinnamon mixed together. Bake at 200°C/400°F/Gas 6 for 10 minutes, then at 190°C/375°F/Gas 5 for 30 minutes. Leave until cold before serving.

SCONES

225g/8 oz self-raising flour
a pinch of salt
50g/2 oz block margarine
25g/1 oz caster sugar
6 × 15ml spoons/6 tablespoons milk

Put the flour and salt into the processor bowl. Cut the margarine into small pieces and add to the bowl. Process until the mixture is like fine breadcrumbs (plastic blade). Add the sugar. With the machine running, pour 5 × 15ml spoons/5 tablespoons milk gradually through the feeder tube to make a soft dough. Knead the dough lightly on a floured surface for 1 minute. Roll out to 2cm/¾ inch thick. Cut out 12 rounds using a 5cm/2 inch cutter. Put the rounds on a greased baking sheet so that they just touch each other. Brush the tops with the remaining milk. Bake at 220°C/425°F/Gas 7 for 12 minutes. Cool on a wire rack.

Variations

Fruit Scones
Stir in 50g/2 oz mixed dried fruit before rolling out.
Cheese Scones
Omit the sugar. Add 50g/2 oz grated or chopped Cheddar cheese with the milk.
Cheese and Onion Scones
Add 1 finely chopped small onion with the cheese and milk. A pinch of dried mixed herbs may also be added.

HONEY LEMON COOKIES

100g/4 oz soft margarine
100g/4 oz caster sugar
1 egg
4 × 15ml spoons/4 tablespoons clear honey
250g/9 oz plain flour
1 × 5ml spoon/1 teaspoon baking powder
a pinch of salt
50g/2 oz chopped mixed candied peel
6 × 15ml spoons/6 tablespoons lemon curd

Cream the margarine and sugar until just mixed (plastic blade). Add the egg and honey and mix until incorporated. Add the flour, baking powder and salt and process to a soft dough. Put heaped teaspoonfuls of the mixture on to a greased baking sheet. Flatten the tops with a fork dipped in cold water. Put a little peel on top of half the biscuits. Bake at 180°C/350°F/Gas 4 for 20 minutes. Lift carefully on to a wire rack to cool. When cold, sandwich pairs of biscuits together with lemon curd, with peel-topped biscuits on top.

PINEAPPLE COOKIES

225g/8 oz canned pineapple rings
225g/8 oz plain flour
1 × 5ml spoon/1 teaspoon baking powder
1 × 2.5ml spoon/½ teaspoon salt
40g/1½ oz lard
6 × 15ml spoons/6 tablespoons peanut butter
175g/6 oz caster sugar
1 egg
12 glacé cherries

Drain the pineapple and chop finely (metal blade). Put to one side. Put the flour, baking powder and salt into the processor bowl. Cut the lard into small pieces and add to the bowl with the peanut butter. Process until the mixture is like breadcrumbs (plastic blade). Add the sugar and egg and mix until smooth. Add the pineapple and mix just long enough to incorporate. Put heaped teaspoonfuls of the mixture on to a greased baking sheet. Cut the cherries into small pieces and put a piece on top of each cookie. Bake at 190°C/375°F/Gas 5 for 20 minutes. Lift carefully on to a wire rack to cool.

VIENNESE WHIRLS

100g/4 oz butter
100g/4 oz block margarine
50g/2 oz icing sugar
175g/6 oz plain flour
50g/2 oz cornflour
grated rind of ½ lemon
12 glacé cherries
extra icing sugar

Cut the butter and margarine into pieces. Add the icing sugar and mix until light and fluffy (plastic blade). Add the flour, cornflour and lemon rind and mix until creamy. Put the mixture into a piping bag fitted with a star nozzle and pipe 24 whirls on to a greased baking sheet. Cut the cherries in half and put a piece in the centre of each cake. Bake at 190°C/375°F/Gas 5 for 15 minutes. Cool on a wire rack. Dust thickly with sifted icing sugar.

CRUMB FINGERS

225g/8 oz plain flour
175g/6 oz block margarine
100g/4 oz sugar
2 × 5ml spoons/2 teaspoons grated lemon rind
a pinch of ground ginger

Put the flour into the processor bowl. Cut the fat into small cubes and add to the bowl. Process until the fat is just rubbed in (plastic blade). Add the sugar, lemon rind and ginger, and process until the mixture is like fine breadcrumbs. Press the mixture into a greased 20cm/8 inch square tin. Press down very lightly with a fork, then bake at 160°C/325°F/Gas 3 for 30 minutes. Leave for 10 minutes and mark into fingers with a sharp knife. Leave until completely cold, then cut into fingers.

SWEET BISCUITS

100g/4 oz block margarine
150g/5 oz caster sugar
1 egg yolk
225g/8 oz plain flour
flavouring (see below)

Cut the margarine into small pieces. Mix all the ingredients, except the flavouring, to a firm dough (plastic blade). Add the chosen flavouring, and process until just mixed. Press the mixture into a greased 17.5 × 27.5cm/7 × 11 inch tin, and bake at 180°C/350°F/Gas 4 for 30 minutes. Cool and cut into squares.

Flavourings

Almond Biscuits
Add 1 × 5ml spoon/1 teaspoon almond essence and 25g/1 oz flaked almonds. Press into the tin and sprinkle with 25g/1 oz flaked almonds before baking.

Coconut Biscuits
Use 175g/6 oz plain flour and 50g/2 oz desiccated coconut with 50g/2 oz chopped glacé cherries.

Ginger Biscuits
Add 1 × 5ml spoon/1 teaspoon ground ginger and 25g/1 oz chopped crystallized ginger.

SAVOURY COCKTAIL BISCUITS

25g/1 oz Cheddar cheese
75g/3 oz butter
225g/8 oz plain flour
salt and pepper
1 × 5ml spoon/1 teaspoon mustard powder
1 egg yolk
3–4 × 15ml spoons/3–4 tablespoons water
50g/2 oz salted peanuts

Grate the cheese (grating disc). Cut the butter into small pieces. Add the flour, salt, pepper, mustard, egg yolk and 3 × 15ml spoons/3 tablespoons water and mix to a firm dough (plastic blade). If the dough looks dry, add the remaining water and mix again. Place the dough on a floured surface and sprinkle with the cheese. Fold over the dough to enclose the cheese and roll thinly. Cut into small shapes with different cutters. Put the shapes on a greased baking sheet, and prick them lightly with a fork. Chop the peanuts finely (metal blade) and sprinkle on the biscuits. Bake at 180°C/350°F/Gas 4 for 15 minutes until golden. Cool on a wire rack and store in a tin.

ALMOND PASTE

225g/8 oz ground almonds
100g/4 oz icing sugar
100g/4 oz caster sugar
1 × 5ml spoon/1 teaspoon lemon juice
1 × 5ml spoon/1 teaspoon almond essence
1 egg, beaten

Mix the almonds, icing sugar, caster sugar, lemon juice and essence just long enough for them to be well blended (plastic blade). With the machine running, add the egg through the feeder tube until the mixture blends into a firm paste. Do not overwork the paste or the oil will run out and discolour any icing placed on top.

Note Two eggs may be necessary if they are small. Egg yolks may be used for almond paste (and the whites used for a royal icing) but this gives a dark yellow paste. For a pale and delicate almond paste, use egg whites only.

FLUFFY ICING

40g/1½ oz unsalted butter
1 × 15ml spoon/1 tablespoon grated orange **or** lemon rind
450g/ lb icing sugar
2 × 15ml spoons/2 tablespoons orange **or** lemon juice
1 × 15ml spoon/1 tablespoon water

Put the butter into the processor bowl with the rind, and cream until just mixed (plastic blade). Add half the sugar and process until mixed. Add the juice and water and the remaining sugar, and continue processing until light and fluffy.

Note The butter should be soft but not melted.

BUTTER ICING

350g/12 oz icing sugar
175g/6 oz butter
flavouring (see below)

Sift the icing sugar and mix with the butter and flavouring until light and fluffy (plastic blade).

Note The butter should be soft but not melted.

Flavourings

Chocolate
Add 15g/½ oz cocoa or 50g/2 oz melted plain chocolate.
Coffee
Add 2 × 5ml spoons/2 teaspoons coffee essence.
Lemon
Add 1 × 5ml spoon/1 teaspoon lemon juice and 1 × 5ml spoon/1 teaspoon grated lemon rind (or a few drops of lemon essence).
Mocha
Add 15g/½ oz cocoa and a few drops of coffee essence.
Orange
Add 2 × 5ml spoons/2 teaspoons orange juice and 1 × 5ml spoon/1 teaspoon grated orange rind (or a few drops of orange essence).
Vanilla
Add a few drops of vanilla essence.

CHOUX PASTRY

100g/4 oz butter
300ml/½ pint water
150g/5 oz plain flour
a pinch of salt
4 eggs

Put the butter and water into a pan and bring to the boil. Tip in all the flour and salt at once and cook gently, stirring well for 2 minutes until the mixture leaves the sides of the pan. Cool for 10 minutes and put into the processor bowl (plastic blade). With the machine running, add the eggs, one at a time through the feeder tube, mixing until completely incorporated. Use as required.

QUICK FLAKY PASTRY

225g/8 oz plain flour
a pinch of salt
150g/5 oz block margarine, well chilled
125ml/4 fl oz cold water, well chilled

Put the flour and salt into the processor bowl. Cut the margarine into four pieces and put one piece into the bowl. Process until the mixture is like fine breadcrumbs (plastic blade). With the machine running, add the water gradually through the feeder tube until a ball of dough forms. With a knife, divide the ball of dough into four pieces while still in the bowl. Cut the remaining margarine into tiny pieces and sprinkle between the sections of dough. Process just long enough to mix in the margarine. Put on to a well floured surface and roll out 5mm/¼ inch thick. Fold over the top and bottom of the dough and half turn to the right. Roll out and fold again, and half turn to the right. Roll out and fold again, and half turn to the right. Roll out once more and fold. Cover and chill for 30 minutes, then roll out and use.

HOT WATER CRUST PASTRY

350g/12 oz plain flour
1 × 5ml spoon/1 teaspoon salt
100g/4 oz lard
150ml/¼ pint milk and water mixed

Put the flour and salt into the processor bowl. Heat the lard and liquid together in a pan until the fat melts. Bring to the boil. With the machine running, pour the hot liquid through the feeder tube and process to make a soft dough (plastic blade). Turn on to a lightly floured surface and knead until smooth and free from cracks. Use while warm to make savoury raised pies.

Note This pastry becomes stiff and difficult to handle as it cools. To keep it warm, wrap in polythene and keep in a warm place.

SUET CRUST PASTRY

225g/8 oz self-raising flour
1 × 5ml spoon/1 teaspoon salt
100g/4 oz shredded suet
150ml/¼ pint cold water

Put the flour, salt and suet into the processor bowl. With the machine running, pour the water through the feeder tube until the dough forms (plastic blade). The pastry should be soft but not sticky, so add the water slowly – you may not need it all. Knead lightly on a floured surface and roll out or form into dumplings.

Note This pastry may be boiled, steamed or baked.

SHORTCRUST PASTRY

225g/8 oz plain flour
a pinch of salt
50g/2 oz lard
50g/2 oz block margarine
3 × 15ml spoons/3 tablespoons cold water

Put the flour and salt into the processor bowl. Cut the lard and margarine into cubes and add to the flour. Process until the mixture is like fine breadcrumbs (plastic blade). With the machine switched on, add the water through the feeder tube to make a firm dough. Roll out and use as required.

Variations
Wholemeal Pastry
Substitute plain wholemeal flour for white flour. It may be necessary to scrape down the bowl once or twice during processing as wholemeal flour tends to fly about the bowl. Add a little more water if necessary as wholemeal flour is a little more absorbent than white.
Savoury Pastry
Add 50g/2 oz grated Cheddar cheese to the flour. Season with a pinch of pepper and a pinch of mustard powder.

PICKLES AND PRESERVES

PICKLED RED CABBAGE

900g/2 lb red cabbage
225g/8 oz cooking salt
1.5 litres/2½ pints vinegar
2 × 15ml spoons/2 tablespoons whole pickling spice

Cut the cabbage into eight wedges and remove the hard core. Shred the cabbage (slicing disc). Arrange alternate layers of cabbage and salt in a bowl, cover and leave in a cool place overnight. Put the vinegar and spice into a pan, bring to the boil and then simmer for 15 minutes. Leave until cold and then strain to remove the spices. Drain the salt liquid from the cabbage. Rinse the cabbage in cold water and drain completely. Pack into hot jars and pour on the cold vinegar to cover it completely. Press down the cabbage with the handle of a wooden spoon from time to time as the vinegar is poured in so that air pockets are eliminated. Seal and label.

Note Keep for a week before using, but do not store the cabbage longer than 3 months, or it will become very soft.

APPLE MINT CHUTNEY

900g/2 lb cooking apples
900g/2 lb onions
450g/1 lb red tomatoes·
8 × 15ml spoons/8 tablespoons mint leaves
3 large sprigs parsley
225g/8 oz sultanas
grated rind and juice of 2 lemons
450g/1 lb dark soft brown sugar
600ml/1 pint white vinegar
2 × 5ml spoons/2 teaspoons salt
2 × 5ml spoons/2 teaspoons ground mixed spice

Peel and core the apples and cut them in quarters. Cut the onions into large pieces and chop with the apples (metal blade). Skin the tomatoes and chop (metal blade). Chop the mint and parsley (metal blade). Put the apples, onions, tomatoes and herbs into a large preserving pan. Add the sultanas. Add the lemon rind and juice to the pan with the sugar, vinegar, salt and spice and stir over low heat until the sugar has dissolved. Bring to the boil, and simmer for about 1½ hours, stirring until the chutney is thick and brown. Pour into warm jars, seal and label.

Apple Mint Chutney

76

MIXED MUSTARD PICKLES

1 marrow
1 cucumber
450g/1 lb French beans
1 cauliflower
450g/1 lb pickling onions
25g/1 oz cooking salt
275g/10 oz sugar
50g/2 oz plain flour
50g/2 oz mustard powder
15g/½ oz turmeric
15g/½ oz ground ginger
15g/½ oz ground nutmeg
1.2 litres/2 pints vinegar

Wipe but do not peel the marrow. Remove the seeds and pith. Chop coarsely (metal blade) and put into a large bowl. Chop the cucumber (metal blade). Chop the French beans (metal blade). Add the cucumber and French beans to the marrow. Break the cauliflower into small pieces and add to the bowl with the skinned onions. Sprinkle with the salt, cover with cold water and leave overnight.

Drain off the water. Mix the sugar, flour, spices and a little of the vinegar to make a smooth paste. Put the vegetables into a pan with the remaining vinegar and simmer until just tender. Add a little of the boiling vinegar to the paste and mix well. Return to the pan and simmer for 10 minutes, stirring well. Put into warm jars, seal and label.

TOMATO PURÉE FOR THE FREEZER

1.8kg/4 lb ripe tomatoes
100g/4 oz bacon, without rinds
1 onion
1 × 15ml spoon/1 tablespoon oil
salt and pepper
a pinch of sugar
a pinch of ground nutmeg
2 bay leaves

Wash the tomatoes but do not peel them. Cut them in eighths and chop coarsely (metal blade). Put to one side. Chop the bacon and onion coarsely (metal blade). Heat the oil in a pan and cook the bacon and onion for 5 minutes, stirring well until the onion is soft and golden. Add the tomatoes and stir over gentle heat for 10 minutes. Add just enough water to cover, and season with salt, pepper, sugar, nutmeg and bay leaves. Cover and simmer until the tomatoes have completely disintegrated and the mixture is soft and thick. Cool slightly and remove the bay leaves. Blend in small quantities until creamy (plastic blade). Put through a sieve and leave the purée to cool. Put into rigid containers and cover, leaving headspace for expansion. Seal, label and freeze.

Note This purée makes a useful base for sauces and is particularly good for sauces to be served with pasta. It may also be used as a basis for soups.

GOLDEN JAM

1.4kg/3 lb cooking apples
1.4kg/3 lb eating pears
1.2 litres/2 pints dry cider
1.8kg/4 lb sugar
$\frac{1}{2}$ × 2.5ml spoon/$\frac{1}{4}$ teaspoon ground ginger

Peel and core the apples and pears and tie the peel and cores in a large piece of muslin. Chop the flesh coarsely (metal blade). Put into a preserving pan with the cider and the muslin bag and simmer for 40 minutes. The fruit should be soft but with some pieces still whole. Take out the muslin bag and squeeze thoroughly to return all the juice to the pan. Stir in the sugar and heat gently, stirring until the sugar has dissolved. Add the ginger and bring to the boil. Boil rapidly until setting point is reached. Cool for 5 minutes, then stir well. Pour into warm jars, cover and label.

CHUNKY MARMALADE

1.4kg/3 lb Seville oranges
2 lemons
3.6 litres/6 pints water
2.8kg/6 lb sugar

Scrub the oranges and lemons and cut them into small pieces, being sure to save any juice. Remove the pips and tie them in a muslin bag. Chop the fruit coarsely (metal blade). Put into a preserving pan with any juice which has run out. Add the water and the bag of pips. Bring to the boil and then simmer for about 1$\frac{1}{2}$ hours until the peel is soft and the quantity of mixture reduced to a half. Remove the bag of pips and squeeze out the liquid into the pan. Stir in the sugar, and heat gently until it has dissolved. Boil rapidly for about 20 minutes until setting point is reached. Remove from the heat at once and leave to stand for 15 minutes. Skim with a perforated spoon, and then stir thoroughly to distribute the peel. Pour into warm jars, cover and label.

INDEX OF RECIPES